BRIDGING WORLDS

··· A Sherpa's Story ···

PEMBA SHERPA WITH JAMES MCVEY

BRIDGING WORLDS

··· *A Sherpa's Story* ···

SHERPA PUBLISHING

Written and published in the United States of America
Authors: James McVey and Pemba Sherpa
Book Design: Jose Yavari

Published by: Sherpa Publications
Boulder, Colorado
www.sherpachai. com/pembas-story

Printed in Nepal
Vajra Publications
Amrit Marg
Kathmandu 44600, Nepal

ISBN 978-0-9855111-4-2

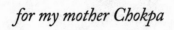

for my mother Chokpa

CONTENTS

FOREWORD

I have known Pemba for five years now, although I can't recall when we actually met. This in itself is neither surprising nor significant given the nature of our friendship and the way it evolved over time, culminating finally in the writing of this book.

Working nights in Boulder, I often found myself with some time to wait before catching the last bus up the canyon to my home in the mountains. Not only was Sherpa's Restaurant conveniently located near a bus stop at the edge of town, but it afforded the relaxed atmosphere conducive to quiet reflection at the end of the day.

In particular, I came to appreciate the Traveler's Library and Lounge, the intimate taproom at the front of the restaurant. Surrounded by adventure books and old climbing gear anchored to the walls, I could imagine myself a solitary traveler far from home. It was common knowledge that some of the Sherpas who worked at the restaurant had stood atop Mount Everest numerous times. Trail runners from different countries frequented the Lounge as well, adding to the international flair.

When Pemba walked into the room, it was hard not to notice. Young, fit, smartly dressed, he carried himself with an easy grace. And yet, watching him in conversation with customers, or speaking Nepalese with one of his staff, I sometimes had the impression that he might rather be running a steep trail behind the Flatirons or climbing a wall in Eldorado Canyon or, as I would later learn, flying his Piper over the Continental Divide.

During one of my regular visits to the Lounge, I must have let it slip that I was an author, because Pemba somehow came to know this and approached me one night to ask about it. He was writing his life story, he said, showing me the callous on his right index finger as proof. While guiding a group of Westerners in Nepal years earlier, he'd watched Sherpa children playing in the street when it occurred to him that he might have a story to tell. I remember thinking there might be some personal matter at the heart of his motivation, something going on internally that perhaps he needed to resolve. But this remains sheer conjecture, as I never asked him directly about it.

Then, in 2015, he was invited to appear on a BBC World radio program with Reinhold Messner to discuss the earthquake in Nepal. During the introductions, he listened as the interviewer referenced the litany of books that Messner had written. Pemba did not have a single book to his name and the omission, at least to him, was glaring.

By this time, Pemba was accomplished in his own right as an alpinist, athlete, and businessman. With his adventure travel business, Boulder restaurants, Sherpa Chai, and real estate holdings, he'd acquired the wherewithal to oversee a number of philanthropic projects in Nepal. All the while, he was raising a young daughter with his wife Mariko. But when he took on the enormous task of raising money and transporting relief supplies to earthquake victims in Khumbu, the demands on his time became too much. The writing project would have to wait.

As it turns out, I'd earned enough of his trust by then that he asked me if I might be interested in writing the book. Although I didn't fully appreciate it at the time, owing to the kind of person he is, the foundation of our friendship had already been set. Our values and intentions aligned nicely. So well, in fact, that the understanding we shared went unspoken.

Bridging Worlds is the product of countless hours of interviews, research, and writing. Although we worked closely throughout the process, Pemba allowed me the latitude and freedom to tell his story the best way I knew how. That required a good deal of trust on his part, something I appreciate. Because Sherpas have experienced so many extraordinary events in recent memory—Everest tragedies, civil war, a major earthquake, dramatic economic and cultural change—I felt compelled to place his story in a broader context. It will be clear to readers the extent to which I have relied upon other journalists and commentators to provide that context.

While it made sense to position Pemba's personal journey in the overall journey of Sherpa people, it came with a risk. The danger, especially for a Westerner like myself, was to insinuate that Pemba's story is representative of the entire Sherpa experience. Like any group of people, Sherpas view the events and circumstances of their lives differently. As compelling as it may be, Pemba's voice is but one in a multitude.

Surely, when he sat down to write his story, he must have felt the urge to reconcile the two worlds he moves between: East and West, poverty and affluence, Sherpa and American. After all, he has made a career of it—pursuing opportunities in the United States, while introducing Westerners to the beauty and wisdom of Sherpa culture.

Pemba is fearless and compassionate, with the courage to act on his convictions. He is dedicated to helping people less fortunate than himself, especially the Sherpas of Khumbu. It should come as no surprise, therefore, that proceeds from the book will go toward improving the lives of people in Nepal.

This has been a beautiful experience for me, made so by the grace and good cheer of Pemba and the many Sherpas I have met along the way.

James McVey
June, 2019

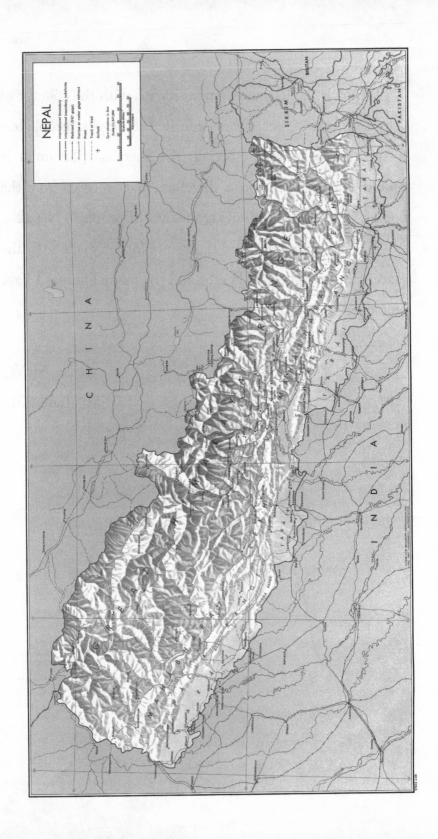

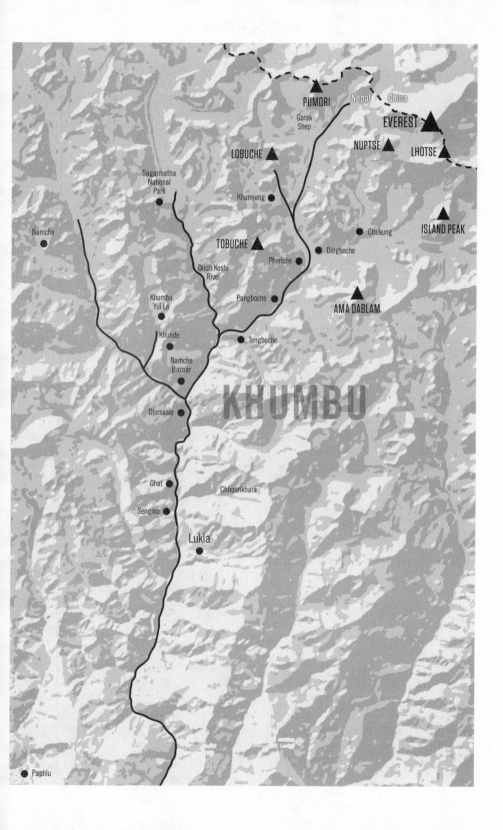

CHAPTER ONE
Early Childhood

I was born in the Everest region of northeast Nepal, not far from the small village of Sengma. I do not know the exact date of my birth, although I believe it was sometime in October of 1971. Like many Sherpa families, we were farmers and herders, grazing our livestock in the mountains above the village. On one occasion, while my father was away, my pregnant mother led the animals to the jungle pastures high above the village. When she went into labor, she walked into the bamboo shelter where she slept at night, and delivered me alone. When it came time to cut the umbilical cord, she couldn't find her knife

My home village of Sengma

and prepared to sever the cord with two stones. Eventually, she found the knife in time. She remained alone with me for three days until my father arrived at the camp.

I lived with my parents and eleven siblings in a stone house without electricity, plumbing, or running water. Our village of Sengma consisted of ten houses perched on a hillside high above the Dudh Koshi ("Milk River") in the Khumbu region, about twenty-three miles from the summit of Everest as the crow flies. The river takes its name from the glacial melt that colors the water. Khumbu is a spectacular place of snow-covered peaks and deep gorges, glacial valleys and forested hills, waterfalls and cascading streams. To this day, there are no roads in Khumbu. Because of the high elevation and cold climate, farming has never been easy. For food, we grew potatoes (the main staple), barley, buckwheat, corn, beans and a variety of greens. We also owned a dozen or so *zoms*—a cross between a yak and a cow.

In late spring, we would drive our livestock to pasture in Lumding. At 14,000 feet elevation, Lumding is a sacred valley rarely visited by Westerners. Surrounded by snow-covered peaks 8,000 meters high, the valley comes alive in summer with blooming trees and wildflowers—crimson rhododendron, the creamy white flowers of magnolia, blue Himalayan poppies, purple primulas, and bunches of white orchids. Most of the

time I went around barefoot with minimal clothing. I remember it raining a lot and being cold, sitting beside a pine and pitch fire to get warm. My mother and sister would be there too.

At home in our kitchen

After a couple of weeks of grazing the livestock in one meadow, we'd move the herd to a different location. At night, we slept inside a canvas shelter, which could be packed up when it came time to relocate to a different pasture. We cooked our meals inside this shelter. We made milk, butter, and cheese, which we would sell every week at the market in Namche Bazaar. At the market, we'd buy different foods to take back with us to the summer camp or to our house. At the end of summer, we'd bring the *naks* (female yaks or zoms) back down to Sengma.

My mother Chokpa

One of my favorite activities as a boy was watching birds. I'd look for them in the forests of rhododendron and blue pine, or in stands of juniper and dwarf birch: finches and warblers, laughing thrushes, and a whole host of colorful pheasants. My favorite was the *danphe*, the national bird of Nepal. Danphes typically live at 11,000 feet elevation or higher. The males have long green crests and beautiful iridescent feathers of copper, teal, and purple. Among the big animals I encountered were red pandas, black bears, and snow leopards. I've only seen a snow leopard a few times in my life, always at a distance, usually among rocks along the side of a mountain. Red pandas, on the other hand, were quite common. I remember always trying to touch one, only to have it run away.

Despite the poverty and hardships of living in Khumbu, Sengma was a wonderful place to grow up. Very few foreigners visited the area, and it still had the feel of an isolated Sherpa kingdom. Strong family relations are important in Sherpa culture, and I was very close to my siblings and mother. Back then, people tended to remain in the village where they were born without the expectation of ever leaving. We were happy with what we had, perhaps because we knew no other way of life. Growing up in Sengma made me appreciate the simplicity of life and meeting the basic needs of food, shelter, and clothing. There were few complications beyond that.

But times change. Today, most Sherpas no longer live in

On the way to Everest Base Camp

Khumbu. I myself left home at fourteen for the capital city of Kathmandu, where I worked for an expedition company as a mountaineer and guide. Five years later, I migrated to the United States and started my own international adventure company. I operated the company for twenty years, traveling the world and meeting many interesting people. Along the way, I earned a pilot's license and learned to fly my own plane. Today, I am a successful businessman living in Colorado where I own two restaurants and eight properties in Boulder. With my wife and young daughter, I enjoy a life of relative affluence. But this only begins to tell the story. Each year, I return to Khumbu, where I am reminded of where my journey began. I have never forgotten the poverty and hardships of my people. As much as I am proud of my personal accomplishments, my story is a people's story. I am both Sherpa and American, walking in two worlds.

For centuries, Sherpas lived in relative isolation as farmers, herders, and traders. Because of its remoteness and inaccessibility, Khumbu remained virtually cut off from the outside world until the mid-1900s, when British climbers turned their attention to Nepal in their effort to summit Mount Everest. Ultimately, this spawned a climbing and trekking industry that would profoundly change the region and transform Sherpa culture. Roughly 3,000 Sherpas presently live in Khumbu, while another 30,000 inhabit small villages scattered throughout the mountains of eastern Nepal. Sherpa commu-

Sherpas farming in Sengma

nities also exist in India, in places like Sikkim and Darjeeling. Today, Sherpa people can be found in all parts of the world including Europe, Australia, and the U.S. More than 5,000 Sherpas live abroad, half of them in New York City. Still, the heart of Sherpa country and culture remains the Solokhumbu—a relatively small region of valleys along the southern slopes of Mount Everest.

Contrary to the assumption of many, a Sherpa is not a porter or mountain guide. The word "sherpa" has been distorted by Westerners to mean a particular occupation in the climbing industry. But this is not accurate. To be a Sherpa is to be a member of an ethnic tribe that settled the Everest region of Nepal roughly 500 years ago, the first people to inhabit this part of the Himalaya. Beginning sometime in the early 1400s, a small group of Sherpa families began a migration from eastern Tibet that would eventually land them in the uninhabited Solokhumbu region of Nepal. The name "Sherpa" speaks to these origins, translated from Tibetan to mean "People from the East." Four main clans, numbering perhaps fifty individuals in all, migrated from Kham in eastern Tibet, bringing with them

A traditional dance at our home in Sengma

the traditions and religion of Tibetan Buddhism. In subsequent years, they would be followed by other Sherpa clans coming from Tibet. Among the highest mountain dwellers on earth, Sherpa people today are known throughout the world as the fabled inhabitants of the Himalaya.

As was the custom in Sherpa culture, my parents were brought together in an arranged marriage. My mother was originally from Hewa—a three-day hike from Sengma. She was hard-working, compassionate, and loving. As a boy, I remember the many rituals she observed in and around the house: putting out seven bowls of water in the morning as an offering to the gods (*yonchap*), swinging a brazier filled with burning incense (*sangbur*), making regular visits to the monastery, and taking time for daily prayers. To this day, she remains a devout Buddhist, living in Kathmandu where I see her regularly.

My father, who grew up in Sengma, was mayor of the area. He was often away from home, leaving my mother alone to care for the children and farm. As mayor, my father was respected throughout the area and people were eager to accommodate him. He was physically very strong. He often brought me with him as he went politicking from village to village. Of all the children, he chose me because he was proud to show me off, even though I was bored most of the time. Sometimes, we'd be stranded in a village for two or three days while people served him cups of *chang*—the local, home-brewed beer. There were times we'd end up in someone's home for the night, and the man of the house would be gone. On one occasion, I remember my father telling me: "you sleep with the daughter, and I'll sleep with the mother." I wasn't sure exactly what he meant by this.

I don't have good memories of my father. He was an abusive alcoholic, often beating my mother. It hurt me emotionally and psychologically to see him hit her. When I was five, I remember thinking to myself that I was not going to grow up to be like him. A year later, my father died after falling from a makeshift bridge into the river, leaving my mother to raise the eight children who remained alive at the time.

Of the twelve children born in our family, only six are alive today. The others died of illness and other causes related to living in poverty and harsh conditions. This rate of mortality was not uncommon among Sherpa children. Of the many dangers we faced on a daily basis, crossing the river was certainly among them. Every year, a new bridge had to be built by villagers after the monsoon runoff swept the existing bridge away in summer. The bridges, made of bamboo, were often dilapidated and unsafe. I myself witnessed a boy named Pasang fall into the river, only to be swept away to his death. I can still recall his parents running downstream, screaming, as other villagers tried to help. The boy's body was never recovered. This tragedy still haunts me, and for years I vowed that, if I ever had the chance, I would build a safe bridge over the river.

My youngest brother Wangdong was born disabled, and

it was my responsibility to feed and care for him. Far from being a burden, this gave me great joy as I grew very fond of him. The feeling was mutual. I remember how he smiled when I came into view. As he became ill, suffering, I convinced my mother to take him to a hospital. I was eleven at the time. The closest hospital was in Khunde at 3,840 meters elevation. The journey was difficult, walking uphill most of the way while carrying a sick child. It took us three days to reach the hospital. All the while, Wangdong grew weaker. He eventually died in my mother's lap. He was five. Instead of returning home with a cured infant, we returned with a dead child. We buried my brother by the river to the chants and prayers of Buddhist monks, as is customary in Sherpa culture for young people who have died. Despite my grief, I see now that his death may have been for the best, not only for him, but also for the family in light of the hardships of our lives.

CHAPTER TWO
Sherpa Spirituality

When people speak of "the Buddha," they're usually referring to the Indian prince Guatama Siddartha who attained enlightenment in the sixth century B.C. Guru Rinpoche, sometimes called the Second Buddha, was an Indian mystic and tantric master who lived in the eighth century A.D. Sometime around 730 A.D., Guru Rinpoche was invited to Tibet for the purpose of introducing Buddhism there. He is credited with being among the founders of the *Nyingma* tradition, the oldest sect of Mahayana Buddhism and the source of Sherpa spirituality.

The Nyingma is based on the original translations of Buddhist scripture from Sanskrit into Old Tibetan. In fact, these written translations mark the first appearance of a Tibetan alphabet and grammar. Among other characteristics, the Nyingma is known for its use of hidden forms of teachings, or *terma*. It also features the practice of *Dzogchen*, which seeks to understand the nature of mind. Finally, the Nyingma allows for the incorporation of local deities and religious practices, as well as elements of shamanism.

During his visit to Tibet, Guru Rinpoche warned that there would be times of conflict when people would be forced to abandon their homes and take refuge in secluded mountain valleys throughout the Himalaya. In anticipation of this, he sanctified a number of places as sanctuaries, including the Khumbu region. Guru Rinpoche instructed that directions to these sanctuaries, or *beyuls*, be written into religious texts, which were then hidden in the surrounding landscape. In difficult times, *lamas* and devout followers could consult hidden teachings in the texts to find directions to the beyuls.

His words proved prophetic. Sometime in the early 15th Century, a number of clans living in eastern Tibet faced trouble in their village of Kham. Rather than remain in Kham and fight, something that was against their religious beliefs, they fled the village and set out in search of a beyul, carrying books with them which described the mountain and valley where they would find refuge. Guided by lamas who deciphered hidden teachings in the texts, they journeyed westward along the north side of the Himalaya.

At the time, the only two ways to enter Khumbu were via a high mountain pass to the north, or along the steep gorge of the Dudh Kosi in the south, making it a naturally protected area. The Sherpa ancestors crossed the Himalaya through Nangpa La Pass, where they found deep snow and glaciers much larger than the ones that exist today. Still, the hardy band of four clans persevered, establishing small homesteads in the lower valley near the present-day village of Lukla. Eventually, a number of families settled the upper valley along its lower slopes.

Sherpa people have always recognized the power of their home. In addition to the spiritual *presence* of the mountains, the extreme landscape makes it difficult and dangerous to live there. Sherpa belief does not seek to conquer or control this power as much as to accommodate it through prayer, ritual, and ceremony. This requires a spiritual resilience on the part of people. According to traditional Sherpa worldview, everything exists both in physical form and spiritual form. As much as a beyul exists as a geographical location, it also exists as a place in the mind. Not only did ancestral Sherpas need the skills and knowledge to decipher the teachings of ancient texts, they also needed a strong faith to recognize certain signs in the landscape to find their way to Khumbu. Spiritual power was required to sanctify the region as a beyul, and it was required to open it as a sanctuary. In this regard, the beyul exists as an inside place, a spiritual sanctuary, whose path demands courage and conviction.

Traditionally, Sherpas believe that the high mountain peaks and passes are inhabited by deities who embody the power of the place. In the heart of Khumbu is the mountain *Khumbila*. Khumbila is short for *Khumbu-yul-lha*, protector of the land, people, and religion. Khumbila rides a white horse, carries a tall banner, and wears the traditional headdress worn by Sherpa men. Another important deity is *Jomo Miyo Langsangma*, ("goddess, mother of the world") who resides on *Chomolung-*

ma—the Tibetan name for Mount Everest. Miyo Langsangma is one of five Long-Life Sisters who inhabit the high peaks of the Himalaya. She rides a red tiger and is very beautiful, adorned in colorful silk cloth and a wreath of flowers that she wears on her head. In her right hand she holds a bowl of food, and in her left, a mongoose that provides good fortune. Since the early 20th Century, many Sherpas have gained wealth by working on climbing expeditions to Everest. To this day, before embarking on these expeditions, Sherpas perform a *puja* ceremony to honor the goddess, asking for her blessing and safe passage as they prepare to enter her abode. Many Sherpas believe that accidents occur when the gods are not honored and given their due respect.

For traditional Sherpas, the practice of religion is a daily exercise. Prayers and rituals are integrated into everyday life, merging the metaphysical with the commonplace. A visitor to Khumbu only has to look at the surrounding countryside to see all the religious objects: prayer flags, prayer wheels, *stupas*, and *mani* stones. Prayers and rituals keep the thoughts of Sherpas on Buddhist teachings, helping them to unify their actions, bodies, and minds. They help bring people into harmony with nature and spiritual powers.

Prayer flags can be seen nearly everywhere on the landscape—strung across rivers and mountain passes, flying from tall staffs and rooftops, draped beside trails and along hillsides. Printed on each flag is a prayer and, in some cases, an image of the wind horse, carrier of prayers. Five colors may be found on the flags as well, representing the elements of earth, wood, water, fire, and metal. Carved mani stones bear a single chant, prayer, or Buddhist image. Prayer wheels, on the other hand, may contain thousands of prayers printed on scrolls. Also found on the landscape are small monuments known as *chortens*. Historically, chortens—otherwise known as stupas—served as memorials for the dead. When the Buddha was asked what should become of his body upon death, he requested that it be placed in a simple stupa. Since then, the stupa has come to symbolize the body, mind, and spiritual development of the Buddha.

Sherpa religious objects contain different levels of meaning and understanding, so that with a simple spin of a prayer wheel or flutter of a prayer flag, anyone with good intentions can earn spiritual merit. Sherpa prayers and rituals are designed to bring about a positive state of mind in people in order to generate spiritual energy for the benefit of all beings. Whether people believe a Buddhist deity is an actual being living on a mountaintop, or merely a symbol of nature's power, it does not really matter. What matters is that through the religious objects, and all the various levels of explanations and meanings in the prayers and rituals and ceremonies, people are reminded that there exists a power greater than themselves.

CHAPTER THREE
School

I started school at age nine in the village of Chhourikhar-ka, located a mile downstream from Sengma on the other side of the river. To get to the one-room schoolhouse, I had to walk a mile and a half *upstream* to cross a suspension bridge, then walk back down the valley to Chhourikharka. The walk to school every morning took three hours. I'd wake at 6 a.m., do a few house chores, pack a lunch, then walk to school where I might get punished for being late. More than once, the teacher would roll up my shirt and whack my arms with a thick bam-boo stick. In the afternoon after school, I would retrace my

A view of Everest from the hills above Sengma

steps and walk the three hours back to Sengma. I had neither shoes nor a coat, and oftentimes I walked barefoot in the rain, negotiating slippery mountainsides, and removing leeches that had attached to my skin.

Because the teachers at school were Hindu, we spoke Nepalese in class and not our native Sherpa language. Nepalese, an Indo-Aryan language, is the official language of Nepal. This is because the vast majority of Nepalis are of Indo-Aryan ancestry. In a nation of 29 million people and more than fifty different ethnic groups, Sherpas make up less than one percent of the total population. Sherpa, like many languages spoken in the northern and eastern parts of Nepal, belongs to the Tibe-to-Burman family, and consists largely of Tibetan words.

As a small ethnic group in Nepal, Sherpas struggle to maintain their traditional culture in the face of outside influence. One tradition that has survived over the years is the method by which Sherpas name their children. I mention this because Westerners are often baffled by the given names of Sherpas—which typically correspond to the days of the week—as well as by the common surname of "Sherpa."

Most Sherpa children are named after the day of the week on which they were born. For instance, "Pemba" is the Sherpa

My family with Sengma in the background

word for Saturday, "Phurba" for Thursday, "Dawa" for Monday, and so on. This method of naming can also be found among Tibetans, especially those living in the Everest region. By naming a child this way, he or she is associated with a protector deity corresponding to that particular day of the week. Thus, Pemba is protected by Saturn, Phurba by Jupiter, Dawa by the moon, etc. Each time the name is pronounced, the relationship between child and deity is reinforced. But this is not the only way Sherpa children get their names. If there is already a child named Phurba in the family, for example, a second child born on Thursday may be named Ang (young) Phurba. Other names may be added as the child grows older. These are typically virtuous names such as "Tshering" (Long life) or "Tenzing" (the holder of Buddha Dharma).

The common surname of "Sherpa," on the other hand, seems to have originated with Nepalese census-takers who assigned a last name to people who only went by one name. Traditionally, last names are not part of Sherpa culture. In some cases, government officials added a clan name to serve the purpose of a last name. In others, the last name simply became the name of the ethnic group (i.e. "Sherpa").

At the school in Chhourikharka, we were taught math, reading, science, history, and economics. Despite all the challenges, I liked school and was good at it. I was especially good with numbers. In my first year, I was selected as the smartest student in the entire school. This included students from four grades. In fact, I held this distinction for all four years I attended the school. There were times when I traded my knowledge for food, offering to help classmates with their schoolwork in exchange for some of their lunch.

By the time I was in my fourth year, however, my mother decided I was needed at home to work on the farm. But I liked to learn and wanted to continue my education. As a boy I was independent and headstrong. If I got something in my mind to do, I was determined to see it through to the end. I studied hard, wanting to be the best.

A teacher from the school traveled to our house on two separate occasions, trying to convince my mother to let me remain in school because I was so smart. But she could not be persuaded. I need my son at home, my mother told the teachers, the first priority is food. In Khumbu, where the need to acquire sustenance was paramount, most of my childhood was spent not in a classroom, but tending crops and gathering fire-wood so my family could cook a hot meal. My four years at the school in Chhourikharka proved to be the only formal educa-tion I ever received.

CHAPTER FOUR
Kathmandu

While attending school in Chhourikharka, I would often see Westerners hiking the main trekking route, with Sherpas carrying their gear. Although I didn't think too much about it, I was aware of expeditions to Everest and the trekking business in general. I suppose it was just a matter of time before I got into the business myself, although how it happened seems more of an accident than anything else.

One of my best memories of this time was receiving my first pair of shoes at age thirteen. I still recall the thrill of running around, jumping from boulder to boulder, not worrying about hurting my feet. The sensation was exhilarating. Perhaps I should have known then where my future would lie.

By the time I was fourteen, I would see young Sherpa men returning from Kathmandu with nice possessions, and, naturally, I wanted to have these things for myself. So, after some planning, I decided to leave home and go to the city. It was autumn, the beginning of the dry season. While tending to the animals in the jungle above the village, I started off on foot for Kathmandu, telling neighbors along the way to inform my mother where I was going. In my small daypack I carried 1,000 *rupees*, gift money that had been given to me by relatives. For food, I brought a bag of popcorn I'd made from corn we fed to the animals.

I followed the trekking route south along the Dudh Koshi River, arriving in the village of Jiri during *Dasain*—a fifteen-day festival celebrated by Nepalis in honor of the goddess *Durga*. A hike that took most people seven days to complete, I finished in three. For a teenager who had never been outside Khumbu, Jiri was impressive. With a hundred stone houses, electricity, and running water, it was the biggest village I'd ever visited. I saw things I'd never seen before, such as a bicycle and a bus.

After spending the night in a tea house, I awoke the next morning and decided to walk through the village. It wasn't long before I came upon a group of boys playing cards and gambling. Thinking I could make some money, I asked to join in. Not long into the game, I found myself losing badly. When I realized I had lost 600 rupees, more than half my money, I became frantic. Then I noticed that one of the boys, a little older than me, was not playing fair.

"Why are you cheating, *Machikne?*" I asked him.

"What did you call me?" he replied.

Then he slapped me in the face.

Outraged, I hit him in the head with a stone, knocking him to the ground. The next thing I knew, the boy's friends surrounded me and started punching me. The police were called and I was arrested. The policemen forced me to walk with them to the station which was an hour away, hitting me all the while with their clubs. I was locked in a dark room for an entire day, my legs shackled to a wooden rack. There were rats in the room, and I could hear them throughout the night. Other prisoners were in the jail cell with me, and periodically they were taken away and beaten by the police. At one point, a policeman looked at me and said, "Your turn is next."

On the second night, I was taken from the jail cell and led to a campfire where policemen were singing and dancing, celebrating the festival. The head policeman seemed to like me.

"Hey, little boy," he said, "would you rather dance or get beat up?"

He gave me food and invited me to join in the festivities. So I danced and sang with the policemen. All the while, I was frightened they might beat me, or lock me up again in the jail cell. After a couple hours of this, the head policeman finally called the parents of the boy from the card game whom I had hit with a stone. After hanging up the phone, the policeman had me sign some papers and then released me. "If you fight again," he warned, "now you know what will happen."

After spending the night in Jiri, I decided the next morning to buy a bus ticket for 60 rupees and continue on to Kathmandu. I still had my popcorn in my daypack. When I arrived in Kathmandu, I was overwhelmed by all the activity at the bus station: the taxis and bicycles and crowds of people, many of whom were speaking languages I did not understand. With only about 200 rupees left in my pocket, I found a cheap place to spend the night, and slept on a concrete floor. I stayed at the tea house for three nights, exploring the city by day. I looked for work but couldn't find a job anywhere, not even as a dishwasher. When my money ran out, I became homeless.

One day, while walking through the city, I saw my cousin, Ang Temba Sherpa, riding a bicycle. After stopping him and explaining my predicament, he invited me to stay with him in his apartment. Ang worked as a senior guide for Great Himalaya, a trekking-touring company based in Kathmandu. With a bicycle and apartment, he was well off by Sherpa standards. He even bought me a new pair of pants and shirt. Feeling a lot better about things, I ended up staying with him for a few months while getting to know the city.

At some point, I asked Ang if he could get me a job with the trekking company. He said there might be an opportunity as a porter. Because I was physically strong, I readily agreed. Not long after that, I was hired as a porter on a trek known as the Annapurna Circuit, which crosses Thorongla Pass at 18,000 feet elevation. Wearing flip-flops and limited clothing, I carried two big duffel bags for a few dollars a day.

As the guide, Ang was responsible for eighteen French clients. At some point during the trek, the clients became curious about me, and so my cousin, who spoke French, told them my life story. Upon hearing my story, one couple wanted to help me get an education, offering to take me with them so I could enroll in a school in France. I was willing to go, but I had no passport or any other document that would allow me to travel internationally. Instead, they graciously lent me $200 (20,000 rupees) so I could further my education in Nepal.

But I was young and irresponsible. When I returned to Kathmandu, I took the money and went shopping for sunglasses, cigarettes, a watch, and other items befitting a teenage lifestyle. Rather than enrolling in school, I continued living with my cousin and working with Great Himalaya. On my next trek, I went as an assistant guide, setting up tents, preparing place settings at meals, and performing other tasks. I had a good job and was making decent money.

CHAPTER FIVE
Everest Climbing History

Sherpas have been involved in Everest expeditions ever since the first reconnaissance mission took place in 1921. By then, Sherpa people were living in communities outside of Nepal in places such as Lhasa, Tibet and Darjeeling, British India. Upon the recommendation of a Scottish mountaineer named Alexander Kellas, a team of British climbers hired a corps of Sherpas in Darjeeling for the 1921 expedition. Kellas, a physician and frequent visitor to the region, recognized that Sherpas were especially adapted to high altitude by virtue of having lived at elevation for centuries. On top of that,

Sherpas had developed a reputation among resident colonialists for being hardworking, congenial, and intelligent. With so many Sherpas living in Darjeeling, the British hired them in large numbers as porters and helpers. Thus began a relationship between Sherpas and Western mountaineers that continues to this day.

Other expeditions would embark from British India in the years following 1921, and it wasn't long before Sherpas living in Khumbu began migrating to Darjeeling to work as load-bearers. The mountaineering industry in the Himalaya was underway, and Sherpas found themselves at the center of it. After centuries of living as farmers, herders, and traders, Sherpa people had discovered an entirely new industry upon which to develop their economy. Since 1921, Sherpas have participated in nearly every Himalayan expedition that has taken place. In that time, mountaineering has played a key role in transforming Sherpa culture and shaping the history of Sherpa people.

Sherpas worked as porters and camp helpers on the first nine Everest expeditions in Tibet, all of which originated in Darjeeling. With Nepal closed to the outside world, the early expeditions had no other choice but to approach Everest from the north. The first eight expeditions were British, each requiring a 400-mile trek across the Tibetan Plateau just to get to the base of the mountain.

From the start, Sherpas distinguished themselves as competent alpinists, capable of extraordinary endurance at high elevation due to their enhanced ability to transport oxygen to the bloodstream and muscles. On top of this, Sherpas endeared themselves to Western climbers because of their dependability, courage, skill, and friendliness. Eric Shipton, a British mountaineer who explored the Himalaya beginning in the 1930s, wrote: "It is the temperament and character of the Sherpas that have justified their renown and won them such a large place in the hearts of the Western travelers and explorers. Their most enduring characteristic is their extraordinary gaiety of spirit. More than any other people I know, they have the gift of laughter."

In 1933, a seventeen-year-old Sherpa named Tenzing Norgay emigrated to Darjeeling, hoping to work on an Everest expedition led by Shipton. Although Tenzing wasn't selected that year, he remained in India and was hired by Shipton for the 1935 expedition. The young Sherpa proved himself to be an exceptional mountaineer, working on numerous expeditions thereafter. By 1947, he'd been on Everest three times.

Then in 1949, the Forbidden Kingdom of Nepal opened its borders to foreigners, ending centuries of isolation. A year later, Communist China closed Tibet to the outside world. Western mountaineers seeking to climb Everest now set their sights on the south side of the mountain. No climbing expedition had ever originated in Khumbu, mainly because Sherpas considered the high peaks of the Himalaya to be the sacred dwelling places of deities who should be honored and respected from afar. The idea that a man could "conquer" a mountain was a foreign concept, part of a mindset introduced by European mountaineers. To this day, climbing remains primarily an occupation for most Sherpas—a way to earn money to support themselves and their families.

In 1953, a British expedition under the leadership of John Hunt launched what would be the third attempt of Everest from the Nepalese side. Although there were only eleven climbers, the expedition rivaled a military operation in the way it laid siege to the mountain, deploying 800 porter-loads from Banepa to the Tengboche Monastery. Porters were paid 93 rupees to make the seventeen-day trek with their loads. Situated on a high point of land above the Imja Khola River, with spectacular views of Everest and Ama Dablam, the Monastery served as base camp for the expedition. The Head Lama at the monastery bestowed his blessing on the climbing party, beginning a tradition that Everest climbers still observe.

Among the climbers on the British expedition was Angtharkay Sherpa, perhaps the most renowned Sherpa climber of his time. Tenzing, who by now had been on seven different Everest expeditions, was also on the team. The year before, he had climbed to within 800 vertical feet of the summit as a member of a Swiss expedition. The two Sherpas were joined by Edmund Hillary, an acclaimed mountaineer from New Zealand, who had been part of a British expedition in 1951 which also failed to reach the summit.

Tenzing and Hillary were selected to make the final ascent of Everest and become the first men to stand on top of the world. On May 27th, the two dug a precarious camp on the Southeast Ridge at 27,900 feet. The next morning, upon emerging from the tent, Tenzing sighted Tengboche Monastery 15,000 feet below and pointed it out to Hillary. With the aid of bottled oxygen, Tenzing and Hillary reached the summit just before noon on May 28, 1953. Hillary took a photograph of Tenzing standing on the summit, holding an ice axe bearing the flags of India, Nepal, Great Britain, and the United Nations. Before starting down on the descent, Tenzing buried chocolate and a few biscuits in the snow as an offering to the gods.

Neither man was prepared for the attention and controversy they would encounter in the wake of their great achievement. Word of their success reached London on the evening of June 1st, a day before the coronation of Queen Elizabeth II. The fortuitous timing only added to the enormous pride felt throughout the British Commonwealth. The Queen promptly made Hillary a knight of the British Empire. Meanwhile, the Nepalese were quick to claim that Tenzing was the first to reach the summit before Hillary. The nationalistic frenzy that greeted the two men on their way back to Kathmandu put Tenzing in an unenviable situation. He and Hillary had agreed beforehand to announce that they had reached the summit together as a team. Hillary, who would become a lifelong friend of the Sherpa people, thought it appropriate that a Sherpa be among the first to summit Everest.

When the expedition team reunited in London for a royal ceremony, Hillary and Hunt were awarded knighthood, while Tenzing received the George Medal—a lesser honor. He could have received the George Cross, a higher award, but this was not the case. Hillary himself felt uncomfortable that Tenzing did not receive knighthood. He believed Tenzing deserved the honor as much as he did. Sherpas, Indians, and most Asians felt that Tenzing had been slighted and not given the recognition he was due. While proud of his accomplishment, Tenzing would regret all the controversy that followed his achievement. At one point, he reportedly told his daughter Pem Pem Tshering: "I wish I'd never climbed this mountain. I think Jomolunghma must have punished me when I come to think of all the politics because I stepped on her head."

The success of the 1953 ascent would not have been possible without Tenzing. The expedition benefited from his experience, knowledge, and skill. In fact, Everest expeditions have always depended on the support and skill of Sherpa alpinists. Since the very beginning, Sherpas have played a fundamental role in helping Western climbers reach the summits of Himalayan mountains.

Today, Sherpas are internationally known for their elite mountaineering skills. They are among the most accomplished alpinists in all the world. In the years since 1953, Sherpas have stood on top of Everest many more times than Western climbers. Perhaps the most renowned Sherpa climber was Ang Rita Sherpa, who summited Everest ten times without oxygen, a feat that was later eclipsed by Apa Sherpa who did it eleven times. In the spring of 1999, Babu Chin Sherpa climbed to the top of Everest and spent a record twenty hours on the summit, all without oxygen. In 2018, Kami Rita Sherpa set the record for most summits at twenty-two, breaking the one he shared with Apa Sherpa and Phurba Tashi Sherpa. In 2019, he scaled Everest twice more to bring his total to twenty-four.

Despite the political complications that followed his historic 1953 ascent and the personal disappointments he may have endured, Tenzing's legacy runs deep. His singular achievement represents a pivotal moment in the history of Sherpas. Overnight, Tenzing became a global sensation and an inspiration for millions of people. The iconic image of him standing on the summit of Everest captivated the imagination of people around the world. From that point forward, the name "Sherpa" gained international recognition and admiration.

CHAPTER SIX
Becoming a Guide

After working at Great Himalaya for a year, I returned to Sengma to visit my family. With money I'd earned from guiding, I was able to buy gifts for my mother and bring them home with me. I ended up staying in Sengma for a few months before returning to Kathmandu to continue working as a guide.

By this time, I was fifteen or sixteen. I'd become self-centered, always wanting things my way. I was rude to my siblings and disrespectful to my mother. I became a bully, hanging out with a gang of teenage boys, picking fights that I knew I could

Working for Great Himalaya at sixteen

win. Frustrated with my behavior, my mother decided to arrange a marriage for me. While visiting her brother in her hometown of Hewa, she saw a girl working in the fields who seemed like a good match.

At this time, perhaps 95 percent of Sherpa marriages were arranged. In the generations before mine, virtually *all* Sherpa marriages were arranged. Today, I estimate the number to be about 70 percent. With more and more education and travel, younger Sherpas are deciding for themselves whom to marry.

When my mother returned from her visit to Hewa, she informed me of her decision. I was open to the idea, thinking I'd now have a girlfriend. I entertained great visions of the girl, and my expectations grew. Satisfied with my response, my mom sent word to her brother in Hewa, who then approached the girl's family with the offer. They were in agreement as well, so my uncle made the arrangements for us to be married. He sent word back to my mother informing her of the good news.

A few weeks later, I prepared to go to Hewa to meet the girl's family. My mother packed a bottle of *rackshi* for me to present to the family as a gift. After walking for two days, I went to my uncle's house in Hewa to announce my arrival. He gave me directions to where the girl lived and I started out for her house. When I arrived, I was greeted warmly by her family. Before I was introduced to the girl, my intended wife, her parents showed their hospitality by offering me tea and something to eat. I was nervous and full of anticipation.

When finally she appeared in the room, I was gravely disappointed. She was not the girl I had envisioned. Shy and demure, she sat beside me, and I knew I had to remove myself from the situation. Meanwhile, her mother was in the kitchen cooking a meal for us. After a few minutes, I informed her father that I must return to my uncle's house for some urgent business. He said fine, thinking I would soon be back. I rose from my seat, placed the bottle of rakshi on the table, and made my farewells. Instead of going to my uncle's house as I had said, I walked all the way back to Sengma.

When I arrived home, my mother asked why I had returned so early. I told her that I didn't like the girl she had chosen for me, and that she was torturing me for insisting that I marry her. She became very upset. Not only was I going against Sherpa custom, but she felt bad for everyone involved—her brother as well as the girl and her family. A few weeks later, I returned to Kathmandu. By then, my mother had sent word to her brother about my change of heart and offered her apologies to the girl.

For the next two years, I worked with Great Himalaya and other companies as an assistant guide, before leading my own treks as a full-time guide at age eighteen. I led treks in Nepal and Tibet lasting anywhere from ten days to two months, guiding mostly European and American clients. I enjoyed taking people to Everest Base Camp because the area was home to me, and I often met people on the trail that I knew. I guided seven trips to Base Camp in all, passing through Arun Valley each time. Arun Valley lies between Everest and Makalu, and offers great views of the region's highest mountains. Besides

Sherpas, this area is home to a number of other ethnic groups including Rais, Tamang, and Lumbus chetree. In addition to these treks, I also enjoyed guiding people through the Lhantang area and around Annapurna.

On Kilimanjaro with Nickson Mushi

Eldorado Canyon T2 5.11

Organizing climbing gear with my daughter Nima

Eldorado Canyon, Red Garden Wall 5.8

At the summit of Chhukung Ri, Nepal

My first CMC group in Nepal, 1993

At the summit of Kilimanjaro, 2000

Soloing ice in Vail, Colorado

Flying over the Rocky Mountains

Sherpa's Adventurer Restaurant

CHAPTER SEVEN
To Colorado

On one trek, I met a young American woman named Jody hiking by herself in the mountains. We began talking, and I soon learned she was living in Kathmandu, working as a teacher for a nonprofit organization. We arranged to meet when we both returned to the city, and it wasn't long before we began a relationship. A short time later, her nonprofit closed its operations, and Jody faced the likelihood of having to leave Nepal. She wanted to remain in Nepal, so we decided to marry in a small ceremony in Kathmandu.

I'd always been curious about the United States, having

My first car in Colorado, 1993

befriended a number of American clients in my years as a guide. My desire to go there and see it for myself was fulfilled in 1991 when, at age nineteen, I traveled to Colorado with Jody. Because she had a job waiting for her in Denver, we planned to stay in the U.S. for a few months before returning to Nepal. I immediately fell in love with the Rockies, finding the same natural beauty I'd grown up with in Khumbu and some of the best climbing I'd ever experienced. I was also able to visit some of my American friends I'd met while guiding.

After six months of living in Colorado, it was time to return to Nepal. But by this time, my wife had become pregnant with our daughter Tsering, so we decided to cancel our return trip and remain in Colorado to take advantage of the better hospitals and medical care.

I was completely illiterate when I first arrived in the U.S., unable to read or write in any language. Although I struggled to learn English and adjust to the new culture, I realized the U.S. offered better opportunities than Nepal. I was ambitious and adventurous, eager to learn and explore. On my way to becoming a U.S. citizen, I wanted to capitalize on the career opportunities here. Consequently, after the birth of our daughter, we decided to make Denver our permanent home.

Just as much as I wanted to pursue my career ambitions, I wanted to explore the Rockies and the climbing opportunities it afforded. At the time, there were very few Sherpas living in the U.S., let alone Colorado, and I didn't know anyone in the local climbing community. Wanting to meet other climbers, I joined the Colorado Mountain Club (CMC) in nearby Golden. As a Sherpa, it was not difficult for me to make friends. Some of the CMC members had been to Nepal, and others were eager to go. It didn't take long before I was approached by a number of climbers asking me to lead a trip in the Himalaya. In 1993, at the age of twenty-two, I guided a group of fourteen Americans on a trek through Chola Pass in Khumbu.

After returning to Colorado, word got out about our adventure, and people from across the U.S. contacted me regarding future expeditions. At the time, there were very few outfitters in the U.S. offering trips to Nepal, not like the hundreds that exist today. And so, in partnership with CMC and International Mountain Explorers Connection (IMEC)—a nonprofit based in Boulder—I organized more expeditions. Before long, I was guiding two and sometimes three trips to Nepal per year, most of them through CMC but also some that were private.

It was at this time that I formed my own adventure travel company, Sherpa Ascent International (SAI). I found that I really enjoyed taking foreigners to the Himalaya and sharing what I knew about the culture and history. I liked meeting new people and, of course, I loved trekking in the mountains. I decided to concentrate on adventures that were relatively safe, where people could enjoy themselves and experience the beauty and culture of Nepal. The trips would feature climbs

Yoga on the summit of Island Peak, 2001

in excess of 20,000 feet in some of the more scenic, less-traveled places of the Himalaya. As a Sherpa, I could provide an insider's look into Himalayan culture and

In the dining tent on a trek, 1993

people. I crafted a number of different trips to Nepal and Tibet that fit this description, always researching the places on my own before organizing the treks. In this way, I found my niche in the trekking industry.

From the beginning, I avoided expeditions to Everest. Even when I was approached to guide small groups on the mountain, I declined the opportunity. I'd seen enough in my early days of guiding to know that I didn't want to take my clients there. I certainly thought about getting involved in the Everest market, given how lucrative it was, and I'm confident I would have succeeded based on my business savvy and the fact that I was a Sherpa with history and roots in Khumbu. But I knew

Building a trail in Colorado as a volunteer

the business of climbing all too well: the big money and egos, the government bureaucracy and corruption, the environmental degradation. I believed an expedition on Everest ran counter to the spirit of climbing—operators competing against one another, risking Sherpa lives in order to get clients to the summit; clients who expected special privileges because of the money they'd spent. I even turned down an opportunity to be part of *Everest*, the 1998 IMAX documentary film directed by David Breashears, who personally called me to join him in Utah during the filming. I declined out of principle, sending my cousins instead.

One of the more popular treks I offered at SAI included an ascent of Island Peak. While not a technically difficult climb, Island Peak tops out at 20,274 feet. I felt it was a "good luck" peak insofar as the weather was always stable, and we successfully reached the summit on every attempt we made. I myself guided this trip eighteen different times.

In 2007, I organized a spiritual and cultural tour of Nepali monasteries and villages that was specifically designed for members of the Shambhala Mountain Center in Colorado. Among the many shrines we visited was the famed Tengboche Monastery. As the heart of Sherpa culture and the center of its religious activities, Tengboche is revered by Sherpas and world travelers alike. Of course, Tengboche served as base camp on the successful 1953 expedition that included Hillary and Dawa Tenzing. Following the expedition, Hillary developed a warm friendship with the abbot of the monastery. Tenzing himself was particularly fond of Tengboche, oftentimes spending his days circling the monastery in prayer. In 1989, I was in Tengboche working on a trek with Great Himalaya, when the monastery caught fire and burned to the ground. Along with others, I entered the burning structure numerous times to retrieve statutes and other religious artifacts that could be saved.

On the approach to Island Peak with SAI

Eventually, SAI organized adventures to other continents. Beginning in 2008, we offered excursions to Tanzania that featured an ascent of Mount Kilimanjaro, as well as a four-day safari in the Ngorongoro Crater—a favorite destination for me personally because of the wonderful opportunities for wildlife photography. We hired between forty to fifty Tanzanians on each of these trips. In Tanzania, I befriended a guide named Nickson Mushi, whom I invited to Colorado so he could improve his English and build his own adventure business in his home country, which, I'm happy to say, he has done.

I am deeply grateful for all the opportunities that SAI provided. It allowed me to make a living at something I love to do. What I am most proud of is the positive impact the company had in the lives of many people. On any given trek, I'd hire between fifty and sixty Sherpa guides and porters, providing them with much needed income. Beyond the economic benefits, SAI allowed me to visit with family and friends in Nepal on a regular basis, while sharing the nation's beauty and culture with people from all over the world.

Over time, this role of bringing people together and bridging cultures became more than just a business strategy. Traveling back and forth between Khumbu and Colorado, I was fortunate to experience the best of both worlds. Immersed in these two different cultures, I gained a unique perspective on each. At some point, it occurred to me that the work I was doing might be important. With all its wealth and generosity and opportunities, the U.S. clearly had a great deal to offer the impoverished people of Nepal. At the same time, I discovered that the Himalayas and Sherpa culture had a lot to offer Westerners. Many of the Americans I took to Nepal came back with a different perspective on life. Most Sherpas there have so little, whereas my American and European clients generally had everything they needed. And yet, it was clear that Westerners found something spiritually rewarding about the people and culture of Khumbu.

CHAPTER EIGHT
Forbidden Kingdom

In order to fully appreciate the Sherpa experience, it is necessary to understand the broader context of Nepalese history. In a word, the history of Nepal is complex, shaped over time by migrations of people from different backgrounds and cultures, culminating finally in a pluralistic society of ethnic, linguistic, and religious diversity.

Perhaps a good place to begin is with the country's natural geography. Nepal is divided into three physiographic zones which run east and west: the southern lowland plains of Terai, the central highlands of Pahad, and the high alpine region of

Himal. Khumbu is located in Himal, the northernmost zone of Nepal situated in the Great Himalayan Range. It contains eight of the world's ten tallest mountains, including Mount Everest, the world's highest peak at 8,848 meters (29,029 feet).

Because of this geographic diversity, Nepal's climate ranges from tropical in the south to Arctic in the north. The diversity of biomes is just as impressive, ranging from tropical savannas along the Indian border, to subtropical and temperate forests in the center of the country, to rock and ice in the Himalaya. Kathmandu Valley, located in the central hill region, is the mostly densely populated area of Nepal with 2.6 million people.

The Nepalese people are descendants of three historic migrations—from India in the south, Tibet in the north, and China and North Burma in the east. The large-scale migrations—especially of Asian groups from Tibet and Indo-Aryan groups from northern India—have contributed to the nation's multiethnic population. Most of the Tibeto-Nepalese groups—the Tamang, Rai, Limbu, Bhutia (including Sherpas), and Sunwar—live in the north and east, while the Magar and Gurung inhabit the west-central part of the country. Nepalis of

Indo-Aryan ancestry (Tarai, Pahari, Newar, Tharus) comprise the great majority of the population. Indo-Aryan ancestry has been a source of prestige in Nepal for centuries, forming the hereditary basis of its caste system.

Neolithic tools discovered in Kathmandu Valley suggest that people have been living in the region for at least 11,000 years. Among the earliest inhabitants were the Kirats in the east-central part of the country, the Newar of Nepal Valley (now called Kathmandu Valley), and the Tharus of Tharu-hat. The name "Nepal" itself was first recorded in texts from the Vedic Age (1500-500 B.C.), the era in which Hinduism was founded.

The earliest well-known rulers were Kirats, whose reign in Nepal Valley lasted from roughly 800 B.C. to 300 A.D. During this time, a number of small kingdoms and confederations emerged in the southern part of the country. One of these confederations, the Shakya polity, produced a prince who would eventually renounce his position to pursue an ascetic life. According to Buddhist tradition, Guatama Buddha, the founder of Buddhism, was born in Lumbini, Nepal in 563 B.C.

Hinduism and Buddhism, two closely related religions,

have enjoyed a remarkable coexistence in Nepal. For example, in national festivals associated with legendary events, both Buddhist and Brahmanic versions are represented. The two faiths even share temples and worship common deities. Hindus tend to be concentrated in areas where Indian culture dominates, whereas most Buddhists live in the less-populated northern areas where there is a strong Tibetan influence. Any differences between Hindus and Buddhists have been minimal in Nepal due to the cultural and historical intermingling of the two belief systems.

Following the Kirata dynasty, a Lichhavi kingdom prevailed in the period between 400 A.D. and 750 A.D. The Licchavi dynasty is noteworthy in that it represents the first time a family of Indian ancestry ruled Nepal Valley. This began a pattern that would repeat itself throughout Nepal's history: Hindu kings claiming high-caste Indian origin, ruling over a population much of which was neither Indo-Aryan nor Hindu. Meanwhile in Tibet, the emergence of a powerful kingdom led to the opening of Himalayan passes to the north, ushering in a new era of trade and cultural exchange across the Himalayas and transforming Nepal Valley into a major commercial center between South and Central Asia.

By the late 8th Century, the Licchavi dynasty was succeeded by a Newar confederacy known as the Nepal Mandala. Newars are the descendants of the many different groups that have lived in Nepal Valley since prehistoric times. As various Indo-Aryan tribes migrated to the valley, they adopted the language and customs of the local population while adding to the overall ethnic diversity. Newar civilization, a blend of different cultures, flourished during this period as the valley's traders came to dominate the Himalayan branch of the ancient Silk Road.

By the 12th Century, the Malla dynasty gained control of Nepal Valley and surrounding areas, maintaining its rule for the next six centuries. Although most of the Licchavi kings were devout Hindus, they did not force Brahmanic social codes upon non-Hindus. The Mallas, on the other hand, did. In the late 14th Century, Malla ruler Jaya Sthiti imposed a legal and social code based on Hindu principles. Although the kingdom controlled trade routes northward to Tibet and southward to India, there were a number of principalities in the surrounding hill areas that were able to maintain their independence.

One of these principalities was Gorkha, ruled by the Shah family. By the early 18th Century, Gorkha began to assert its power in the hills to the point of threatening Malla rule in the valley. In 1769, the Gorkha ruler Prithvi Narayan Shah conquered the Mallas and established his capital in Kathmandu. By occupying several small principalities, the Shah achieved the unification of the country and, in so doing, laid the foundation for the modern state of Nepal. In order to maintain political control over a large area characterized by ethnic diversity and regional differences, Ghorka rulers invited local elites into the central administration in Kathmandu.

Once the Ghorka rulers secured a unified Kingdom of Nepal in the central Himalaya, they sought to expand their influence across the entire hill country from Bhutan to Kasmir. But a series of wars with China, the Sikh kingdom in Punjab, British India, and Tibet thwarted their efforts, limiting the Kingdom to the current boundaries of Nepal.

In the early stages of the Anglo-Nepali War (1815-16), the British suffered a stunning defeat at the hands of Gurkha soldiers, earning Nepali fighters an international reputation as exceptional warriors. Among the concessions made by Nepal at the end of the war, British India was granted permission to recruit Gurkha soldiers for military service. This authority to recruit Gurkha soldiers was extended in 1860 when the British conquest of India forced the Kingdom, now ruled by the Rana family, to negotiate with the British in order to maintain its independence. Under the terms of the agreement, the British promised to protect the Rana regime against foreign enemies and to respect its autonomy regarding domestic affairs. In return, the British were allowed to recruit Nepalese soldiers for their prestigious Gurkha units in the British Indian Army. The reputation of Gurkha warriors continued well into the 20th Century, during both world wars and various U.N. peacekeeping missions. Most of the Gurkha soldiers in the British army came from Magar, Gurung, and Rai groups.

As much as it had to accommodate British India, the Rana dynasty was careful to maintain friendly terms with China and Tibet to the north, not only for economic reasons, but also to contain British influence in South Asia. As a result, Nepal was never colonized during this period. Rather, it functioned as a buffer state between Imperial China and Colonial India.

In the period between 1775 and 1951, politics in Nepal

was largely determined by rivalries involving the presiding royal family and competing noble families. Each faction sought political power to the detriment and exclusion of rival groups. Consequently, the political scene in Nepal was driven by family loyalty over and above service to the crown or nation. This history of factionalism and rivalry would set the tone for politics in Nepal for decades to come.

CHAPTER NINE
Sherpa Ascent International

On the many trips I guided through the years, I enjoyed meeting people from all over the world and learning about their life experiences. Unfortunately, not all the lessons I learned in the guiding business were positive. For instance, I came to realize how the attitude of one person can adversely affect the mood of an entire group. Sometimes all it takes is one malcontent to compromise the experience for everyone. The disagreeable person may be overly fearful or needy, but it seems there are some people who can never be satisfied—demanding to be pampered and waited on, expecting to always have their bags carried and meals prepared exactly to their liking. The group might be hiking or camped in a beautiful place, and there will be one person who complains about being miserable. In the presence of a difficult client, I often think about the porters—one or two of whom might be standing close by with heavy loads, wearing flipflops and minimal clothing—and how composed they remain.

Tragedy is another experience that forces one to reflect. In all the years of operating SAI, we lost only one client. For me, the death became a lesson in the importance of communication. On any trek or expedition, it is crucial that guides and clients remain in close communication with one another, especially regarding matters of health. In this case, it may have saved a life.

Sometime around 1997, I led a group of eleven Americans on a classic, three-week Himalayan trek. After summiting Kala Patthar Peak (18,000 feet), we descended and prepared ourselves to climb Island Peak. One client, Peter, was a Polish emigrant who lived in Los Angeles. From the moment I met the group in Kathmandu at the start of the trip, I noticed that he was unusually quiet and withdrawn. He remained quiet on the descent from Kala Patthar, keeping to himself, and it occurred to me that he might be sad about something. Despite my efforts to draw him out in conversation, I couldn't get him to talk very much.

We rested in the village of Dingboche before starting out for Chhukhung. When I noticed that he was walking slowly, I asked if something was wrong to which he replied that he was simply tired. I offered to take him down to a lower elevation, but he said no, that he just needed to rest. Once we arrived in Chhukhung, I put him in a tent to sleep before departing with six clients to climb Island Peak. The rest of the group stayed behind in Chhukhung. I guided the six clients to a high camp where we spent the night at 18,500 feet.

The next day we awakened at 2 a.m. to summit Island Peak, fortunate to have calm winds and good weather all the way to the top. As we began the descent, however, one of the clients experienced acute altitude sickness. He kept falling down in the snow, until I literally had to carry him off the summit back to the high camp where I and others helped him into a tent. We gave him a hot drink until he revived, and we all continued down, arriving that evening in Chhukhung

Biking Karo La Pass (16,304')

at 10 p.m. It was a long work day for me, made even more difficult by the young man who had fallen sick.

When we arrived in Chhukhung, an assistant informed me that Peter had collapsed and died. He might have suffered a heart attack, or his death might have had something to do with the altitude, no one knew. My assistant informed me that the body had been taken to Dingboche by another assistant.

After some hot soup and tea, I made the two-hour hike to Dingboche in the dark. When I arrived, I knocked on the doors of ten different lodges, trying to locate Peter's body. Finally, I learned that the body had not been taken to Dingboche, but to the village of Pheriche instead. By now, it was 1 a.m. and I was exhausted, so I spent the night in Dingboche.

In the morning, I walked to Pheriche where my assistant had delivered Peter's body to the Himalayan Rescue Association Hospital. After checking on the body, I sent my assistant back to Chhukhung to be with the clients. Alone with Peter and his gear, I searched for his passport and eventually found it in a pocket of his travel pants. I then called the U.S. Embassy in Kathmandu to inform them of the situation. Embassy personnel arrived in a helicopter an hour later. After loading all of Peter's gear, I returned to the hospital to carry his body to the waiting helicopter. But the corpse was stiff by then, and I couldn't get it through the cargo door. With the engine going and the rotor blades whirring above, the pilot in the cockpit yelled, "Quick, put it in!" Finally, I had to bend and break the body to make it fit through the door. Once the helicopter departed, I returned to Chhukhung to rejoin the group. Later, in a ceremony near Kathmandu, we cremated the body in the jungle at the wife's request.

At its peak, SAI operated up to six trips per year in such places as Nepal, Tibet, India, Bhutan, and East Africa. Whereas I once guided all the trips, I eventually hired professional Sherpa guides to lead some of the adventures. After more than twenty years of running the business, I found myself becoming interested in other opportunities. The more I pursued these other

At the Kopan monastery with SAI, 1998

interests, the more my attention to guiding suffered. The turning point came while leading a trek in Nepal. Preoccupied with business matters back in the U.S., I realized I was not giving full attention to my clients. Because of this, I decided I could no longer continue as a guide, and so I ended SAI operations in 2014.

As the owner of a successful business in the adventure industry, I was fortunate as a Sherpa to go beyond the traditional occupation of porter to become both a guide and company operator. I am also proud to have succeeded in the industry while pursuing my original vision of featuring adventures that combined alpine trekking with cultural immersion. I felt then, and still feel, that in the Khumbu region the two go hand in hand. To approach the Himalaya as strictly a physical challenge is to overlook the spiritual dimension of the experience—something that runs counter to my beliefs. In light of the many problems that plague the Everest climbing industry today, I feel that a spiritual and ethical respect for the

At the trailhead to Kilimanjaro in 1999

mountain is badly needed.

Although I find myself pursuing other business interests now, no longer devoting my energies exclusively to climbing and guiding, I still remain active in mountaineering. This is my first love, and it always will be. I've been a professional mountaineer for thirty years, climbing throughout the Himalaya and in parts of South America, Europe, and East Africa, encountering some of the most challenging alpine terrain in the

Mount Kilimanjaro

world—falling into crevasses, buried in avalanches, suffering frostbite on all my toes and fingers. I've climbed most of the major Himalayan peaks, reaching summits above 20,000 feet on at least twenty-five different occasions. Since 1991, I've guided forty-nine trekking, climbing, and volunteer-service trips to the Himalaya, introducing hundreds of people to this part of the world. I've guided trips elsewhere in Asia as well as in Africa, summiting Mt. Kilimanjaro five times.

My thirst for adventure extends beyond climbing and trekking. I once bicycled from Lhasa to Kathmandu over the course of eighteen days, crossing a number of high passes. At the border between Tibet and Nepal, I made a bungee jump of 500 feet into the Bhote Koshi River gorge, the longest freefall in the world. If professional mountaineers are said to be competitive in nature, always looking for the next challenge, then I am no exception. My competitiveness has

Running the Denver International Marathon

recently led me to the sport of running, having finished a 5k race in just over fifteen minutes. As an ultra runner, I've competed in a number of marathons in Colorado.

But now, my quest for challenges has taken me in a new direction.

Restaurant business

Boulder's Pemba Sherpa, a 15:17 5K runner who was born in the Everest region of Nepal, has taken over the building formerly housing Nancy's and opened "Sherpa's." The restaurant, at 835 Walnut, features food for athletes. Sherpa runs from the restaurant up Mt. Sanitis every day.

CHAPTER TEN
Sherpa's Adventurer Restaurant

In the early years of operating SAI, I envisioned opening a coffee shop where people could come together to share
information on climbing and traveling. I figured I could use
the space to advertise SAI trips for those who might be interested in visiting Nepal. Because Boulder was widely known
as an adventure and travel destination, I decided to focus
my attention there. When I discovered that the city lacked a
restaurant that offered authentic Himalayan food, it occurred
to me that this might make more sense as a business opportunity. I was still committed to the idea of a community

gathering place for travelers and adventurers, but I began to think more in terms of a full-service restaurant. It seemed to me that a restaurant could provide the same opportunity to achieve the broader vision of bringing people together and bridging cultures. When an old Victorian house on Walnut Street became available, the dream became a reality. In 2002, I opened Sherpa's Adventurer Restaurant.

From the beginning, I envisioned a place that would introduce people to the food, adventure, and culture of the Himalayas. I wanted to serve quality food at an affordable price, while providing a unique atmosphere consistent with the original idea of attracting local adventurers and world travelers. Seventeen years later, I believe we've stayed true to this vision.

Today, Sherpa's Restaurant is one of the most successful restaurants in Boulder, offering a range of traditional Nepalese, Tibetan, and Indian cuisine. All the food is made-to-order by our two chefs who make every attempt to serve only organic meats and fresh vegetables. The cozy dining rooms and white tablecloths accentuate the gorgeous woodwork and large turn-of-the-century windows inside the house. When the weather is warm, we serve food outside on the flagstone patio with spectacular views of the Flatirons—Boulder's iconic rock formation.

As much as it specializes in Himalayan food, the restaurant brings a piece of Sherpa culture to Boulder. This is part of the reason why people come to the restaurant. Perhaps this is best exemplified in the barroom, which we've named the Traveler's Library and Lounge. The room features historic photographs and folk art from the Himalaya, as well as a small library of mountaineering and adventure books. Retired climbing equipment hangs from the walls, including an old ax that once belonged to my father. Traditional Nepalese music plays overhead. One of the beers on tap in the lounge is named Sherpa's Ale, a locally brewed beer made especially for the restaurant.

The restaurant staff consists of twenty-six people, about half of whom are Sherpa. Many have been here since the restaurant opened. Some of the employees are permanent residents of the U.S., while others are here on work visas. Four of the staff have either climbed Everest or worked on Everest expeditions. Jangbu Sherpa, one of our head chefs, has summited Everest ten times without the aid of supplemental oxygen. He has climbed nearly all of the fourteen 8,000 meter peaks in the Himalayas, including K2, the second highest peak in the world. While he may not be known in many parts of the world, Jangbu is revered in Nepal as a mountaineering legend. Another employee, Tashi Sherpa, has climbed Everest eleven times. Soon, the restaurant staff will include Dawa Yangzum, the first Nepalese woman to summit K2.

I take great satisfaction in knowing that I've played a part in improving the lives of others, especially my fellow Sherpas. If I can create economic opportunities for people, or mentor young Sherpas to get started on a career that makes them financially independent, then I am grateful. I understand that my success in business makes this possible.

As a businessman, I am always looking for an opportunity. When real estate values in Boulder started to skyrocket in the 1990s, I began to research the market for its investment value. Gradually, I was able to purchase residential properties located in desirable neighborhoods. Many of the houses needed work, which I was willing to pay for, but it was their location that was most important. Once they were renovated, the houses provided homes for some of the employees at the restaurant. Today, I own eight properties in the city of Boulder including the Victorian house on Walnut Street. Just as I thought they would, the property values have all increased substantially.

In business, I follow a specific strategy that, while not complicated, involves a degree of calculated risk. It begins with a vision of the future based on existing trends and desirable outcomes, followed by a commitment to see the vision through to fruition. Perhaps my biggest asset is tenacity, a trait that served me well growing up poor in Khumbu. When I set my mind to something, I work hard to achieve the objective, and do not give up until the goal is met. Among the principles that guide me in business are recognition, pragmatism, trust, professionalism, and reflection. Use your intelligence to understand how things work, be sure that what you are pursuing has a social value, rely on your passion and street-smarts to achieve the vision, act professionally, and never stop evaluating the process.

Maximizing profit should not be the sole motivation. I believe helping others and building community are key to a successful business, values I attribute to my Sherpa heritage. I am proud of the community we have fostered at the restaurant and the sense of family that includes not only Sherpas, but local folks and travelers alike. My vision of building bridges across cultural lines has taken root. More than once, I have been pressured by adjacent landowners who, like myself, have been approached by the Marriott corporation offering to purchase our properties for the purpose of building a large hotel and conference facility. Despite the substantial windfall I could realize from the sale, I continue to decline the offers because I believe strongly in what we've been able to accomplish here.

CHAPTER ELEVEN
Civil War

I could not have had the success that I did without the help and support of others. Among the people who helped me at critical moments was my cousin, Ang Temba Sherpa. Wandering homeless on the streets of Kathmandu at age fourteen, I was fortunate to cross paths with him in what would become a life-changing moment. He not only rescued me from the streets and provided me with a place to live, he started me on the path to success by arranging a job for me in the trekking industry.

I had great respect for Ang Temba and wanted to repay

him for all he'd done. We had stayed in communication over the years, even after I moved to the U.S. With my early financial success at SAI, I had the means to pay for him to come to the U.S. for a visit. He was still living in Kathmandu when I reached out to him with the offer.

By then, however, Nepal was involved in a civil war. The war, which lasted from 1996 to 2006, was fought between the government and the Communist Party of Nepal (CPN). Led by a group of Maoist rebels, the CPN sought to overthrow the Nepalese monarchy and replace it with a People's Republic. The Nepalese Civil War was the culmination of years of political conflict in the country, going as far back as the British withdrawal from India. Viewed through the lens of history, it came about as a result of the difficult transition from monarchy to democracy, as well as bigger political forces being played out across the entire region of South Asia.

When the British conquered India in 1860, it formed an alliance with Nepal's reigning government, promising to protect the Rana regime against foreign and domestic enemies. But when the British withdrew from India in 1947, it left the tyrannical Rana kingdom vulnerable to opposing political parties inside Nepal, which were all part of a broad democratic movement. This began a prolonged struggle between the monarchy and pro-democracy forces that would last for decades.

In 1950, a settlement was reached between the opposing sides that allowed for power-sharing in the government. But after China invaded Tibet in 1951, India decided to exert its influence in Nepal's internal affairs by backing King Tribhuvan as the nation's new ruler, alongside a government comprised mostly of the revolutionary Nepali Congress Party. In 1959, after years of political wrangling, a new constitution was adopted that established general elections for a national assembly.

But the transition to a more democratic political system remained elusive. A year after the 1959 constitution was adopted, King Mahendra (Tribhuvan's successor) suspended the Nepali Congress government and imprisoned most of its leaders. Mahendra then enacted a new constitution in 1962 that recognized the crown as the legitimate source of authority in Nepal. Mahendra was eventually succeeded by his son Birendra, who assumed control of the throne in 1975. By 1979, a second wave of democratic opposition emerged to challenge his monarchical rule. Birendra responded by allowing a popular election of the National Assembly, while reasserting the royal authority established in the 1962 constitution. But the compromise proved unsuccessful. By 1990, a coalition of opposition forces pressed hard for political reforms, forcing King Birendra's hand. A new interim government was appointed, and the constitution was amended to allow for both a constitutional monarchy and a multiparty parliamentary system.

Adding to the turmoil of this time was the fact that the democratic movement itself was divided by competing factions. If the Nepali Congress Party held sway in the early years, the emergence of the CPN in the nineties tipped the balance. Led by militant Maoist rebels, the Party used violent tactics in its fight to overthrow the monarchy. Tensions escalated until the country found itself in an all-out civil war by 1996.

The violence and chaos of this period was marked by a massacre at the royal palace in 2001, in which King Birendra was killed along with most members of the royal family. The alleged assailant, Crown Prince Dipendra, was reportedly upset after his parents refused to accept a woman whom he had chosen to be his wife. According to reports, Dipendra died three days after the massacre by suicide. In the wake of these events,

Birendra's brother Gyanendra assumed control of the throne.

Meanwhile, the Civil War dragged on. In 2005, King Gyanendra took it upon himself to defeat the violent Maoist campaign by asserting full executive power. By then, however, the war had entered a stalemate. Whereas the Maoists controlled large rural areas of the country, the military held the largest cities and many towns. Finally, in September of that year, the Maoists declared a cease-fire in order to negotiate an end to the war.

Ultimately, King Gyanendra ceded power to the democratic movement, and the House of Representatives was reinstated. Empowered with its new authority, the House voted to curtail the power of the monarchy and declared Nepal a secular state. The days of the Hindu Kingdom were over. On May 28, 2008, the constitution was amended to officially recognize Nepal as a democratic republic, bringing a close to two centuries of royal rule.

In the end, the Civil War claimed the lives of 19,000 combatants and civilians. Another 150,000 people were displaced. Thousands of people simply disappeared and were never heard from again. In 2004, when the Maoists announced a blockade of Kathmandu, which at the time was controlled by the government, the capital city descended into fierce fighting that went on for a year. There were reports of rebels killing civilians who refused to pick up arms and join their cause.

When I hadn't heard from Ang Temba in quite some time, I became worried. Through a journalist friend of mine in Nepal, I placed an ad in a Kathmandu newspaper asking if anyone had any information on my cousin's whereabouts. But I never received a reply. Ten years passed before his family performed funeral rituals on Ang Temba's behalf—a formal recognition that he likely had died. The circumstances of his disappearance remain a mystery to this day, although I suspect he was killed by the rebels. His body was never recovered.

CHAPTER TWELVE
The Legacy of Edmund Hillary

When I was a young student, Edmund Hillary made an appearance at our school in Chhourikharka. His charitable foundation, the Himalayan Trust, had given money to help finance the building of the school. It was a special moment for me to present him with a silk *khata*, a ceremonial scarf of greeting and blessing. Most people know Hillary for his successful summit of Mt. Everest in 1953, but few are aware of his philanthropic work in Khumbu. I have always admired Hillary for all that he did for people in the Solokhumbu region. He remains an inspiration to me, not only for his lifelong work on behalf of Sherpas, but because of the way he went about it. He was a man of action, and his respect and affection for Sherpa people were genuine.

Hillary first visited the Himalayas in 1951 as part of a British reconnaissance mission to climb Everest. He came away with a favorable impression of Sherpa people: "Few of us had failed to learn something from the character and temperament of the men themselves, their hardiness and their cheerfulness; their vigour and loyalty; and their freedom from our civilized curse of self-pity." Hillary attributed these qualities to the hardships and dangers of living in Khumbu.

After his ascent of Everest in 1953, Hillary returned to Khumbu in 1960 to lead an expedition designed to study the effects of high altitude on human physiology. One night, seated around a campfire near Tolam Bau Glacier, he asked his Sherpa friends how he could help their villages.

For Sirdar Urkien, the answer was clear. "In the mountains we are as strong as you—maybe stronger," he replied. "But our children lack education. Our children have eyes but they cannot see."

At that moment, Hillary resolved to build a school for

Sherpa people. "It would be the least I could do for my good friends," he later wrote.

The following year, Hillary returned to Khumbu to oversee construction of a schoolhouse in Khumjung—the first project of international aid in the entire region. But it would not be easy. The building materials would have to be transported from Kathmandu on the backs of porters, a trek that required seventeen days. As luck would have it, a Swiss pilot by the name of Captain Schrieber approached Hillary about flying relief supplies to Tibetan refugees who had fled their homes in the wake of a brutal crackdown by the Chinese Red Army following the 1959 uprising in Lhasa.

Hillary told the Swiss pilot about a primitive airstrip in the Mingbo Valley that might be suitable for landing a small airplane. Hillary offered to organize the clearing of the landing, and asked Schrieber if he could also transport building materials for the Khumjung school. The Swiss pilot agreed. In addition to relief food for Tibetan refugees, Schrieber flew supplies for the schoolhouse into the valley. The building materials were then carried by porters to Khumjung.

Once construction was completed in Khumjung, the villages of Thami and Pangboche inquired whether they too could acquire schoolhouses. Hillary obliged, leading the effort to build schools for both villages in what is remembered as the Himalayan Schoolhouse Expedition of 1963. All construction materials were transported by porters from Kathmandu.

During the 1963 expedition, Hillary witnessed the death of a Sherpa girl who had contracted smallpox. Aware that the contagion could spread rapidly, he and others quickly arranged for an airdrop of vaccine that was promptly administered to hundreds of people in the nearby villages. The outbreak was eventually contained. Hillary later acknowledged that of all the projects that took place during the 1963 expedition—schools, waterworks, medical clinics, etc.—the one that was most appreciated by Sherpas was the vaccination.

Following the 1963 expedition, Hillary set out to build more schools in Khumbu, as well as a hospital in Khunde and a bridge over the Dudh Kosi. To help organize and fund all the projects, Hillary and his wife Louise set up an international charitable foundation in 1964 called the Himalayan Trust. A valued partner in the early years of the Trust was Sirdar Mingma Tsering Sherpa, who organized the labor and materials required for the various projects. Mingma remained an important figure in the Trust and a close friend of Hillary's, until his death in 1994.

The Trust forced Hillary into a new role of fundraiser. He proved up to the task. On one occasion, Hillary appeared before a group of executives at Field Enterprises Educational Corporation, publisher of *World Encyclopedia* and sponsor of the 1960 expedition to Nepal. Expecting him to arrive with lawyers and accountants, one of the executives later recalled that he was surprised when the world-famous climber showed up alone—a tall lanky man with rugged features, carrying an old briefcase held together by twine. When asked how much compensation he wanted for himself, Hillary responded by saying that he personally didn't take money on such expeditions. Up to that point, the executive had never understood why Hillary hadn't cashed in on his fame and become a millionaire. Now he knew. After the Board agreed to Hillary's request for financial support, the executives presented him with a new briefcase.

Certainly one of the biggest challenges for Hillary and his team was getting construction materials from Kathmandu to Khumbu. As it was, the effort took over two weeks and involved hundreds of porters. To solve this logistical problem, Hillary and others purchased a plot of land in Lukla (9,200 feet) on behalf of the Nepalese government, and built a small airstrip. To compact the surface of the landing strip, fifty Sherpas walked and danced their way across the ground for two days.

When the airstrip opened in 1964, Lukla quickly became Nepal's busiest mountain airfield and the preferred gateway to Mount Everest for Westerners. In the years ahead, the airfield would have a profound effect on the entire Solokhumbu region. After all, the valley had been virtually isolated from the rest of the world for centuries. Hillary worried that the influx of tourists might overwhelm traditional Sherpa culture. And while some Sherpas shared his concern, Sherpa people learned quickly to take advantage of the new economic opportunities.

In 1966, construction on the hospital in Khunde was completed. The hospital is still in operation today and treats roughly 9,000 patients a year. With support from the Himalayan Trust, a second hospital was built in the village of Paphlu in 1975. Improved health care remains a top priority for Sherpa people. Although smallpox has been eradicated in Nepal, other deadly diseases persist: hepatitis A, diphtheria, tetanus, typhoid, and polio.

During this time, Hillary became involved in the formation of Sagarmatha National Park. While the idea of a national park had been discussed for some time, a United Nations forester approached Hillary in Kathmandu and asked whether the New Zealand government might help in making it become a reality. Hillary agreed to speak with New Zealand officials, and ultimately played a role in convincing them to take part in the project. In 1975, the two nations reached an agreement whereby New Zealand park managers came to Khumbu and assisted local leaders in developing the new park. In 1976, with support from Hillary's foundation, Sagarmatha officially became a national park, encompassing Mount Everest and the valley systems settled by Sherpas. Three years later, it was designated a World Heritage Site. Today, the Park is staffed by Sherpa wardens, and features a visitor center, three park lodges, and a tree nursery in Teshinga.

Sadly, tragedy struck in 1975 when Hillary's wife Louise and their 16-year-old daughter Belinda were killed in an airplane crash on takeoff in Kathmandu. The destination of the flight was Paphlu, where a second airfield had been built in Khumbu. The bodies of Louise and Belinda were wrapped in white cloth and cremated beside the Bagmati River, the holy river of Kathmandu. The tragedy marked the beginning of many difficult years for Hillary. Although he threw himself into his work in Khumbu, he continued to grieve the loss of his beloved wife and daughter.

Never a Buddhist himself, Hillary remained respectful of the spirituality at the center of Sherpa life. Hillary's foundation provided support to build the Salleri Monastery, and helped to restore other monasteries in need of repair. Through the years, he maintained a close friendship with the abbot of Tengboche Monastery, the site of the first base camp in 1953. In 1989, when the monastery was destroyed by fire, Hillary traveled around the world to raise money for its restoration. Sherpas themselves raised $50,000 in the campaign. After four years of work, all of it done by hand, construction on the monastery was completed.

Hillary's work in Solokhumbu became a lifelong commitment. Year after year, he returned to the region to build schools and health clinics, bridges and waterworks. Four months out of the year, he traveled the world to raise the $1 million needed by the Trust to fulfill its mission. At least thirty schools have been built in Solokhumbu with funds provided by Hillary's foundation, including the school in Chhourikharka that I attended as a boy. Until his death in 2008, Hillary regularly visited Khumbu to check on his projects and see old friends. About his philanthropic work on behalf of Sherpa people, he wrote: "Whereas gratitude has something of inequality about it, goodwill is an active and growing idea that a proud man need not feel ashamed to entertain."

The legacy of Hillary lives on after his death. Following the 2015 earthquake, the Trust was quick to provide emergency shelter and other essential support for impacted communities in Solokhumbu. The Trust also provided temporary classrooms for thirty schools that were either damaged or completely destroyed. In the wake of the 2014 avalanche on Everest that killed sixteen Nepalese workers, the Himalayan Trust established a fund to support the families of the victims, including a scholarship program ensuring that their children would receive a full education.

CHAPTER THIRTEEN
Service in Khumbu

With the continued success of Sherpa's Restaurant, I turned my attention to improving the lives of people in Nepal. At first, I donated money that went toward building trails, schools, and medical facilities in the Khumbu region. Then I became more hands-on, transporting clothes and other materials—including solar panels—on my frequent trips to Nepal. I worked with nonprofit agencies, especially those dedicated to preserving the environment and culture of the Himalaya.

Then in 1999, while guiding a group of Americans, I happened to mention my longtime goal of building a permanent suspension bridge across the Dudh Kosi River near Sengma. Seated around an open fire at a Khumbu lodge, I explained to the group how every year between the months of May and September, torrential monsoon rains raised the river beyond its banks, destroying the bamboo bridge below Sengma. Every year, villagers had to rebuild the makeshift bridge once the monsoon floods receded. The temporary bridge near Sengma was particularly unsafe. This was where I witnessed a boy fall into the river and die as he was swept downstream. I explained to them how each morning as a child, I had to walk three hours to cross the suspension bridge in Ghat in order to get to my school in Chhourikharka, and how a number of children in Sengma simply did not attend school because of the six hours of walking it required each day. Children were missing school, and families were moving away because of the long trek. I was determined to see that a permanent bridge be built at Sengma, because I knew how important education was to the future of Sherpa people.

Among the clients seated around the fire that evening was a man from Portland named Ken Stober. He asked me how much money it would take to build a permanent suspension bridge. Because I had already done the research, I told him that it would cost somewhere in the neighborhood of $20,000. Ken believed so strongly in the project that he offered to donate the money needed to complete the bridge. When he returned to the U.S., he made his donation to International Explorers Connection, a nonprofit organization, which then made the money available to me.

I consulted with an engineer in Nepal, who told me it would take three years for the government to complete the project. Rather than relying on the government, I decided to organize the project myself—hiring a private engineer to complete the final design, purchasing all the concrete necessary for construction, lining up an MI-17 Russian helicopter to deliver the materials and fly the steel cable across the gorge. The cables were anchored into rock on each side of the river. With a crew of eighteen workers, construction on the 300-foot-long bridge was completed in just four months. New trails were cut to connect the bridge to villages on both sides of the river.

When the bridge was finished in December of 2000, Ken returned to Sengma for the celebration party. Building the bridge had been a lifelong ambition of mine, but it was

Ken's generosity that made it happen as quickly as it did. Because of the bridge, the walk to school for Sengma children now takes only thirty minutes. Truancy at the school has fallen dramatically, and families that had moved away have since returned. For the people of Sengma and elsewhere on that side of the river, the bridge provides easy access not only to the school, but to the markets in Lukla as well.

People living in Khumbu face many challenges, including the lack of electricity. In 2007, with monies donated by me and others, a small-scale hydro-electricity facility was built in Sengma. The hillside upon which the village sits provided a slope to harness the energy of a waterway flowing into the gorge below. This quick-fix operation provided enough electricity to intermittently power a number of light bulbs in the village.

Being able to help my friends and family with these kinds of projects brought me great satisfaction. I could see that I was contributing directly to the improvement of their lives.

Meanwhile, having been divorced from my first wife Jody for a number of years, I met a woman in Boulder with whom I fell in love. Mariko and I were married in 2006. Five years later, she gave birth to our daughter Nima. My business was thriving, I was becoming more involved in humanitarian work, and I was recently married with a young daughter. My life seemed complete.

CHAPTER FOURTEEN
My Mother Visits the U.S.

It had always been my hope that my mother Chokpa would visit the United States before she became too old. That hope became a reality in 2002 when, at the age of eighty, she flew from Nepal to Colorado on a journey that took nineteen hours. It was the first time in her life that she had ever been outside the Khumbu region.

Needless to say, the experience was like nothing she had ever known. She had never seen a toilet before, let alone a television or highway. She was overwhelmed by the immense size of the streets and buildings. I took her to a shopping mall, the first she had ever seen. We spent a lot of time cooking at home, something I enjoyed very much. I drove her to the top of Mount Evans and then to Eldorado Canyon, where she watched me climb a multi-pitch wall, prompting her to ask why I would do such a crazy thing. When I showed her the room at home where I stored my climbing gear, she thought that I must surely own a climbing shop and asked where it was located.

My mother had always been the center of our family, the source of strength and love, and it made me feel good to present her with this once-in-a-lifetime adventure. I was fascinated watching her navigate a world that was so foreign to anything she had ever known. As a parent, the experience reminded me of learning to see the world anew through the eyes of a young child. But she was no child. This was a woman of *eighty years*, experiencing new and wondrous things for the very first time. It made me appreciate how incredibly different this world was from all she had ever known in Khumbu. At that moment, I could feel my experience reflected in hers, just as I knew that her life would always be part of mine.

Four years earlier, I had led a group of Americans on a

climbing and trekking adventure in Nepal. Among them was a young computer consultant from San Diego named Mike Salomon. An ice climber, Mike was ascending a 900-foot wall at 20,000 feet when a blinding snowstorm swept in and trapped him on the ice. After bringing him down, the guides could see that he was suffering from dehydration and hypothermia, so we took him to Sengma where he could be nursed back to health. Mike stayed in Sengma for five days, cared for by my mother and others in the village.

Afterward, Mike would recall his five days spent among Sherpas in Sengma. "What I remember most is the way they put me first. Whatever food they had, whatever milk they got, they insisted that I eat before them. They had so much hospitality. And they wanted nothing back."

Mike was impressed by the congeniality and good cheer of the people he encountered. Despite their hardships, he noticed that they never lost their sense of humor. "I never saw any acrimony. They don't seem to know they are lacking anything. Some of the older ones, they don't even particularly seem to want anything. They make do. It's what they've always done."

The bonds between Mike and the Sherpas he met in Sengma became so strong that my family decided to adopt him as one of our own. Not only that, he met a Sherpa woman named Dhaki whom he eventually married. The couple currently lives in San Diego with their two daughters.

His experience in Sengma became life-changing in other ways. When he returned from Nepal to his home in San Diego, he quit his job and started his own consulting company. He named the company Sherpa Technology Guides, setting aside a percentage of its annual profits to go toward helping the people of Sengma. He encouraged other San Diego companies to follow his example by adopting their own Nepalese villages in the area around Everest. One firm, Mires Design, sponsored a project to plant 40,000 trees near a village devastated by the over-harvesting of timber.

During her visit to the U.S., I took my mother to see Mike and the people at Mires Design. We took part in a slideshow at an REI store where she answered questions from the crowd. She wore traditional Sherpa clothing the entire time. In a ceremony at Mires Design, Chokpa thanked the company president in traditional fashion by presenting him with a khata. The pine saplings donated by the company helped reforest parts of

Khumbu, which had been ravaged over the years to build lodges and other facilities for tourists.

While we were in San Diego, Mike took us to La Jolla Cove and Sea World. A reporter from the San Diego Union-Tribune accompanied us as part of a newspaper article he was writing about my mother's visit. In La Jolla, Chokpa walked out on the sea wall, mesmerized by the Pacific. She'd never seen an ocean before. Convinced that it was a holy place, she prayed to it again and again. She wanted to know how big the "lake" was and where it ended. I explained to her that it was an ocean, and that it ended on the other side of the world. She looked at me in disbelief. Later, I showed her the ocean on a map, but this made little difference. She'd never seen a map before.

As we walked along the sea wall, she worked her prayer beads and took in the sights. The smell of the seals surprised her. Worse than yaks, she said. A fisherman let her look in his bucket. Although it was her first glimpse of a fish, she declined his invitation to touch it. The next day at Sea World, she was bolder when trainers brought her a few dolphins to pet. She wondered out loud why they didn't have fur.

In the end, Mike said she came away with the same impression of San Diego that he'd had of Sengma. "She thought it was magic," he said.

CHAPTER FIFTEEN

Tragedy on Everest

On April 18, 2014, an avalanche on Mount Everest killed sixteen Nepali workers, thirteen of whom were Sherpas. It was the deadliest day in the history of climbing on Everest. In fact, there had never been sixteen deaths in an entire season, let alone a single day. The avalanche occurred at 6:30 a.m. when a massive *serac* broke off a hanging glacier on the west shoulder of the mountain above the Khumbu Icefall. Weighing approximately 62,000 tons, the serac fell 1,300 feet into the Icefall where Sherpas were hauling gear from Base Camp to Camp II. At the time, there were 150 Sherpas along the route. One group in particular had gathered near a crevasse, waiting for a ladder to be fixed. Workers had just completed repairs when the serac, the size of a ten-story apartment building, swept down the mountain, cutting a swath a hundred feet wide through the route.

The Khumbu Icefall represents the first real challenge to climbing Everest, and one of its most dangerous ascents. Towering above the Icefall is a mile-high face that buttresses an enormous hanging glacier. As the glacier migrates downward, it calves from time to time, starting ice blocks crashing through the Icefall. Meanwhile, the Icefall itself creeps downhill from Camp I (19,900 feet) to Base Camp (17,600 feet) at a rate of a few feet per day, churning and fracturing into walls of ice and deep crevasses.

Each spring, a group of Sherpas known as the Icefall Doctors is hired by the government to establish a route through the Icefall, fixing ropes and setting aluminum ladders over crevasses and along cliffs. Once the route is set, Sherpas carry bottled oxygen, water, food, tents, and other gear to Camp II and higher. Because warmer daytime temperatures make the ice less stable, Sherpas climb through the Icefall at night, carrying loads of equipment up the mountain. Expeditions on Everest take up to eight weeks to complete because of the time it takes for Western clients to acclimatize to the thin air. This requires an extraordinary amount of gear to be hauled up the mountain, work that is performed by Sherpas.

When rescuers arrived at the impact site following the avalanche, they found the surviving Sherpas already engaged in emergency rescue. Amid the gear that was scattered across the impact zone, they discovered the half-buried body of Dawa Tashi who was alive but unconscious, clipped into a fixed harness. After rescuers dug him out, they noticed another set of legs in the hole. Upon recovering that body, they found yet another. And then another. In all, ten dead Sherpas were found buried on top of one another in the hole, clipped into the same line. Only Dawa Tashi, who was badly injured, survived. Among the dead was Ang Tshering, the oldest of the crew at fifty-six. A veteran of Everest expeditions for over twenty years, this was to be his last season before retirement. He had only to complete this ascent through the Icefall to Camp II and then return to Base Camp. Ang's body, the seventh found in the hole, was identified by his son Pemba Tenzing who was at the scene.

Helicopters were flown up to the Icefall, returning with lifeless bodies dangling from long lines. The bodies were flown to Namche Bazaar, where they were inspected by police to determine a cause of death. The police reports were then sent to an insurance company in Kathmandu as proof that each man had died climbing, thereby qualifying the beneficiary to collect on the policy provided by the expedition operator. By the end of the day, thirteen workers were confirmed dead in the avalanche, and another three were still missing. As for the bodies that weren't recovered, to say a man is "missing" often makes it difficult for the beneficiary to collect payment from the insurance company. At that point, it becomes necessary to gather eyewitness accounts testifying that the man wasn't lost, but rather entombed on the mountain.

But collecting on an insurance policy only tells part of the story. When a Sherpa dies, according to Buddhist tradition, he or she undergoes *bardo*—a transitional period lasting forty-nine days in which the soul lingers close to the body for three weeks before gradually moving away toward a state of reincarnation. To facilitate this transition, the family brings the body of the deceased home with them, where it lies for three days before cremation. The family will talk near the body and place food before it. People of the village visit the house, bringing money and food. Buddhist monks visit as well, meditating and praying. In return, the family presents *gewa* to the visitors in the form of rice, butter, and money—gifts intended to enhance the prospects of reincarnation for the deceased.

If, on the other hand, the body of the dead is not recovered, then the burial rituals cannot be fully performed and the deceased cannot easily reincarnate. In this case, it is believed that the spirit never finds peace. Thus, the body of a Sherpa who has fallen to his death in a crevasse is thought to have a restless spirit nearby.

In the aftermath of the avalanche, a four-day halt was declared for all expeditions so that rescuers could continue to search for the missing three. Perhaps a hundred Sherpas gathered at Base Camp to console one another, their grief mixed with anger. The tragedy brought long-simmering resentment to the surface, especially among younger Sherpas who wanted to cancel the season. "We must respect the dead!" someone yelled. "The route has become a graveyard!" When the government offered to pay $400 to the grieving families, on top of the $10,000 insurance payments, Sherpas considered it an insult. As Grayson Schaffer reported in *Outside* magazine, what followed was a complicated sequence of political wrangling that involved Sherpas, expedition companies and their clients, and the Nepali government. For Sherpas, it became a reckoning of sorts.

At the center of Sherpa discontent were two main grievances: the exceptional dangers they face as expedition workers, and the relatively low wages they earn in light of the $43 million collected annually by the government from expedition companies. For many years, the central government in Kathmandu has been under fire for the way it oversees the Everest industry. The government sells as many permits as it can each year to maximize revenue, and then leaves it up to operators to decide how to conduct and manage the expeditions. A full third of the money generated in the Everest industry goes to the government, and it's not known where the royalties go. For many Sherpas, the government seems only concerned about taking its cut while expedition workers assume all the risk.

Just two days after the avalanche, a group of Sherpas met inside a tent at Base Camp and crafted a list of demands in what became known as the 13-point charter. Among other things, the charter called for accidental-death insurance payouts to be increased from $10,000 to $22,000. The charter also demanded $10,000 in disability coverage for workers permanently injured in the mountains, a $1,000 funeral stipend, a permanent relief-and-education fund to be taken from 30 percent of the government's permit royalties, a memorial in Kathmandu to honor the sixteen who died, and official recognition of the tragedy by making April 18th a national holiday. Nearly 300 Sherpas ended up signing the 13-point charter at Base Camp.

One of the most contentious issues on the mountain was the question of whether to continue the climbing season in the wake of the tragic events. Although the charter stated that any expedition that had Sherpa consent could go forward as planned, the overall feeling, at least initially, was that no Nepali in Base Camp wanted to continue. After witnessing the avalanche and what followed, some may have feared for their own safety. Others didn't want to climb out of respect for those who had died. And then there were those who didn't want to continue as a form of protest to gain better working conditions.

On top of all this, there was intense pressure from their families back home not to climb.

On the other hand, mountain workers knew how critical the season's wages were. Sherpas work in one of the highest-paying industries in Nepal, and this is how they support their families the rest of the year. Not only were they concerned about the specter of lost wages during the Everest season, they also didn't want to jeopardize their positions with the expedition companies going forward.

Given the complicated situation they faced, the majority of Sherpas seemed unwilling to get involved in the dispute. At least not publicly. Part of this reluctance may be attributed to cultural factors. Sherpas, especially those from an older generation, are apt to avoid conflict with Westerners. After all, the Sherpa reputation was built on a cooperative spirit and loyalty to company operators. One climber and restaurant owner in Namche Bazaar put it this way: "You're brought up in a culture where you treat Westerners with great hospitality." Whereas some Sherpas at Base Camp were willing to admit that they didn't want to climb, or that their families were terrified for their safety, others were more circumspect about what they wanted to do.

In the days following the avalanche, the Sherpas aimed their anger squarely at the central government in Kathmandu. Rather than approach their employers—the expedition companies—for higher pay or improved conditions, the Sherpas directed their grievances at the Nepali government, which has long been plagued by dysfunction and corruption. For years, the government has repeatedly neglected or ignored the concerns of Sherpas, while capitalizing on their labor. Consequently, when the government did not immediately respond to the demands outlined in the 13-point charter, the anger at Base Camp intensified. There were open calls to close the mountain for the season. Rumors circulated that threats of retaliation were made to Sherpas who wanted to continue with the expeditions.

On April 23rd, the government finally agreed to send tourism minister Bhim Prasad Acharya to talk with the Sherpas. The next day, the minister spoke to a crowd assembled at Base Camp, assuring them that he would present the 13-point charter to the cabinet. He also declared that any expedition wanting to go forward that year could proceed. At one point, he said: "You Sherpas decide if you want to continue the season."

It was clear that nobody wanted to take responsibility for shutting down the mountain—not the clients who had paid a nonrefundable sum of anywhere between $18,000 and $75,000, not the expedition operators who were in the business of getting people to the top of the mountain, and not the government who feared that the millions of dollars they made on permit fees would be jeopardized.

At least one western operator, Russell Brice, founder of Himalayan Experience, placed the blame on four or five "militant" Sherpas who allegedly were behind the threats of retaliation. Brice told his clients that Sherpas working for him had been threatened with bodily harm, saying that both he and Sirdar Phurba Tashi were angry that the "militants" had effectively cancelled their expedition. In fact, Phurba denied that he had been threatened, saying only that Sherpas did not want to climb that year. Sumit Joshi of Himalayan Ascent, a Nepali expedition company, had this to say: "Western operators knew in their hearts their Sherpas did not want to climb but they couldn't express that clearly to their clients, so they blamed the militants—it's just an excuse to put the blame on somebody else. If this tragedy doesn't change anything, nothing ever will." After all was said and done, the 2014 climbing season was cancelled, and it was Sherpas who made that happen. According to Ed Douglas, longtime British journalist: "They had a choice and in the end they chose respect for themselves and the mountain ahead of money."

Rather than putting the blame on a handful of renegade workers, as some may want to do, I believe it is more accurate to view the events at Base Camp as a case of Sherpas taking control of their own destiny. Always a proud and resourceful people, Sherpas have become more confident and outspoken. No longer content to assume a deferential role in the expedition industry, they understand the value of their skills and contributions. Today, Sherpas are taking a leadership role in the industry. In fact, over half the clients who had contracted to climb Everest in 2014 had done so with Nepali companies. In the words of Douglas: "Tenzing gave the name 'Sherpa' a currency that will never be exhausted, so it may be only now that they're beginning to take advantage of it."

CHAPTER SIXTEEN
Everest Expedition Industry

The following year, just as climbing got under way, an earthquake triggered an avalanche that swept through Base Camp, killing nineteen people including ten Sherpas. Among the dead was a cousin of mine who was working on the mountain. For the second year in a row, the climbing season on Everest was cancelled.

The tragedies in 2014 and 2015 brought many issues to light, exposing the dangers and inequities inherent in the Everest industry. It is true that Sherpas work in one of the highest-paying industries in Nepal, and it is also true that climbing

Everest is dangerous. This has always been the case, and it always will be. Furthermore, given the global interest in climbing Everest and how much money is involved, it is unrealistic to expect the expedition business to end anytime soon. Still, as it is carried out now, the Everest industry is fraught with problems that need to be addressed.

To understand the state of the industry today, it is necessary to remember the history of how it has evolved over the past century. Since the very beginning, Sherpas have played an integral role in the industry, working primarily as load-bearers and camp helpers, participating in virtually every Everest expedition since the first reconnaissance mission in 1921. After Communist China closed Tibet to the outside world in 1950, climbers looked to Nepal which had recently opened its borders to foreigners. The successful British campaign in 1953 not only made international celebrities of Tenzing and Hillary, but it introduced the Khumbu region to the entire world. Following the 1953 expedition, there would be other successful ascents of Everest in 1956, 1960, and 1963. When the airstrip in Lukla was completed in 1964, it made Mount Everest more accessible to climbers and trekkers alike, opening Khumbu to international tourism and putting an end to centuries of isolation.

If in the 1950s there might be on average one Everest expedition a year, that all changed in the coming decades. Beginning in earnest in the 1970s, the mountain saw a steady increase in the number of expeditions. The industry really took off in the 1990s, marked by a growing presence of commercial expeditions. In 1996, the year in which fifteen people died on Everest, there were thirty different expeditions on the mountain, ten of which were conducted by for-profit commercial companies. The number of commercial operators on Everest would only increase in the years ahead.

In addition to the steady increase in expeditions, the way the mountain was climbed had changed as well. If in the old days, everyone on the mountain shared in the work, the commercial companies now took care of virtually everything. In his 1999 memoir titled *View from the Summit*, Hillary commented on the changes:

> "We worked together as a team, established new routes and overcame most problems as they occurred. We climbed roped together, as we believed this was a

safer and more responsible method. Procedures
are very different nowadays …. Increasingly the
mountain is littered with scores of aluminum
ladders and thousands of feet of fixed rope.
Deep tracks are beaten up the mountain by dozens
of eager feet. Even on the Hillary Step near the
summit there is usually a choice of three ropes to
ascend. If the weather is kind, the standard routes
on Mount Everest are far easier now with the
advantage of modern technical equipment. Many
inexperienced people have been conducted to the
summit by expert professional guides."

From the beginning, it's been Sherpas who have done most
of the work: establishing the routes, breaking the trails, lay-
ing the ropes, hauling the loads, setting up camps, cooking the
meals, rescuing imperiled climbers. In order to properly acclimatize to the high elevations, expedition members spend weeks
on the mountain during which time Base Camp becomes a
bustling village, complete with amenities and luxuries. Because
the government doesn't permit equipment to be flown up the
mountain, everything that goes into building all the camps and
supporting the climb—oxygen, food, tents, etc.—has to be car-

ried up. By doing all this work, Sherpas help Western climbers conserve their energy in order to enhance their chances of getting to the top of the mountain. Because of the traits that have endeared them to Westerners over the years, Sherpas are excellent at providing a positive climbing experience. And because of the way the industry has evolved, it would be impossible for the vast majority of Western climbers to summit Everest without Sherpa support.

The growth of the expedition industry has led to a number of problems. Chief among them is overcrowding. Each year, roughly 1,200 people attempt to climb Everest. In 2018, 715 people reached the summit—476 from the Nepal side and 239 from the Tibet side—breaking the record of 667 set in 2013. With more and more clients on the mountain, traffic has increased to the point that bottlenecks of crowds form in the "death zone" above 8,000 meters, where climbers must wait for the path to clear. The more time climbers are forced to wait at that elevation, the more susceptible they become to frostbite and altitude sickness.

In addition to causing long lineups and unnecessary delays, overcrowding on the mountain has compromised the quality of the experience for many climbers. This is particularly true given the number of wealthy clients who are barely qualified to be on Everest, and who would have no chance of successfully climbing the mountain without the services of a guide. The increase in creature comforts at Base Camp and Camp II contributes to the problem. Some have likened the scene at Base Camp to a circus, with an increasing number of Westerners coming up with different ways to attract attention. In 2014, the year of the tragic avalanche, a Hollywood feature film was scheduled to be shot on Everest. Another man planned to fly off the summit in a wingsuit. In 2018, a man died during a publicity stunt for a cryptocurrency. "Everest is no longer a wilderness experience," mountaineer Graham Hoyland recently said. "It's a McDonald's experience."

And then there are the environmental problems. Mount Everest has become littered with human waste, empty oxygen bottles, broken tents, tin cans, food wrappers, and as many as 200 corpses which remain on the mountain. In an article published in 2013 in *National Geographic*, Mark Jenkins wrote: "The two standard routes, the Northeast Ridge and the Southeast Ridge, are not only dangerously crowded but also disgustingly polluted, with garbage leaking out of the glaciers and pyramids of human excrement filled in the camps." Hauling trash and bodies off the mountain is both dangerous and expensive work. As Jenkins explains, "Even under the best conditions, climbing the tallest mountain in the world is exhausting, dangerous work. Dropping used supplies on the mountain rather than carrying it with them can save vital energy and weight.... But the accumulated trash is still steadily ruining one of the most unique places on Earth."

Each year, roughly 700 climbers spend nearly two months on Everest, getting acclimated to the elevation by making regular visits to the four camps above Base Camp. There are tents and other essential gear at these camps, but no toilets. Human waste, deposited in holes dug in snow, has been accumulating for years. Nepalese officials recently warned that human waste left behind by climbers poses a threat of spreading disease.

Meanwhile, the number of inexperienced climbers who are permitted on the mountain continues to be a problem. Overcrowding and marginally qualified members compromise the safety for everyone, especially Sherpas who are weighed down with heavy loads. The situation is made worse when inexperienced climbers sign on with low-cost expedition operators who have been known to cut corners when it comes to equipment and emergency training—this according to Ang Tshering, former president of the Nepal Mountaineering Association. Such operators may also be less inclined to speak out when their clients are unqualified to meet the demands of the mountain. They also are less likely to have the resources to take care of their workers and their families in the event of an accident.

Western guiding companies have long dominated Nepal's expedition industry, but that has changed in recent years with a new generation of Sherpas who have started their own companies. Sherpas have always done the lion's share of the work on Everest expeditions; it only makes sense that some would want to run their own business rather than work as an employee for a foreign company. Over twenty Nepalese guiding companies are now operating on Everest, about the same number as Western companies. On average, local operators charge less than their Western counterparts, somewhere in the range of $20,000 to $50,000 for guided expeditions. In comparison, Western companies typically charge between $35,000 and $75,000, and as much as $130,000 for climbers who want a Western guide.

Not surprisingly, the competition between Western operators and the influx of new local operators is fierce. Tashi Sherpa, managing director of Seven Summits Trek, argues that local operators are well positioned to offer a good climbing experience because of their knowledge of the mountain. Western guiding companies counter that they have a better safety record and a higher percentage of successful ascents. At least one Western operator, Garret Madison, owner of Madison Mountaineering, warns that climbers should be aware that companies offering lower rates may be providing inferior services. Tshering agrees, arguing that the government needs to be more vigilant. "Low-paying means low quality of services: low quality of skill, man power. It's a risk. People must not look only at prices," he says. "Safety and security is most important." Regulating unscrupulous companies and unqualified mountain guides may be the biggest challenge facing the industry today.

According to Jennifer Peedom—documentary filmmaker and director of the 2015 movie, *Sherpa: Trouble on Everest*—rules and regulations on Everest are "fairly nonexistent." In the absence of a well-regulated industry, climbers and expedition operators are left to fill the void when it comes to establishing safety norms. Without an effective policy and protocol in place, safety concerns will continue to be a problem. And it's working Sherpas and other local Himalayans who bear the brunt of the risk. The story of Sherpa deaths on Everest is as old as the industry itself. Ever since 1922, when seven Sherpas were killed in an avalanche during the second British expedition, a disproportionate number of Sherpas have died on Everest. Some 293 climbers have perished in all—175 members and 118 Sherpas. These totals do not include the eleven who have died so far in 2019.

A big part of the danger faced by Sherpas occurs in the Icefall, where they carry loads of equipment up the mountain. It's not uncommon to have dozens of Sherpas traveling through the Icefall at once, walking across ladders placed precariously over crevasses, constantly under the threat of falling seracs and avalanches. In any given season, a working Sherpa might pass through the Icefall thirty different times, compared to two or three times for most clients. Of the many reasons why Sherpas face higher risks on Everest, this is the biggest.

All of which raises the question: how much risk do workers need to take to help foreigners climb Everest—a feat they could not achieve on their own without the overwhelming support from Sherpas and other Himalayans?

In the absence of effective regulatory oversight regarding worker safety and compensation, economics and politics will continue to dictate how these and other questions are answered. Despite the dangers posed from overcrowding and inexperienced climbers, the Nepal government places no limits on the number of permits it issues. Expedition operators, on the other hand, are motivated to get as many of their clients to the summit as possible. Their reputations and business success depend upon it. Clients, of course, pay tens of thousands of dollars for the chance to stand on the summit of Everest, and there's an expectation that comes with paying all that money.

Meanwhile, Sherpas are caught somewhere in the middle—between a viable livelihood and the risks of working on Everest. After the 2014 tragedy, Phurba Tashi, who lives in Khumjung, reflected on the dilemma: "I like doing this work. Everyone from my community benefits, not just in mountaineering jobs but as porters and hotel owners ... everyone makes some money.... Some people believe we are walking on the head of Chomolungma but I don't think of it that way. When I reach the top I say a prayer and I give thanks."

Sherpas who learn technical climbing skills and work high on the peaks—especially those who have summited Everest—enjoy great esteem in their communities. On the other hand, those same climbers stand a fair chance of losing their lives. After the 2014 tragedy, Phurba relented to his family's wishes and decided to retire from climbing. "If foreigners stop coming to Nepal," he said, "I'll survive by farming cattle like my father and grandfather. If there hadn't been the accident, I'd have climbed Everest for the 22nd time. But if my family isn't happy, there's no benefit in earning that money. I would rather not have the record and live with a healthy body and a happy family. So I will stop climbing now."

Depending on their jobs, Sherpas can make up to $6,000 working on a two-month expedition. The higher they work on the mountain and the more they carry, the more they are paid. The pay structure for a Sherpa working for a Western operator might look something like this: a gear allowance of between $2,000 to $3,000 at the start of the season, $15 per day as a base rate, $20 per load to Camp II, $30 to Camp III, $50 to the South Col, and a $500 to $800 bonus for summiting the mountain. Roughly 200 Sherpas get to the top of Everest in an average year. Sherpas who don't make as many carries, or who work for smaller local outfitters, might earn $2,000 to $3,000. A typical expedition might have twelve to eighteen staff openings for Sherpas, with the most desirable positions going to six or so skilled climbers.

Whereas $6,000 represents roughly ten times the average annual pay in Nepal, it hardly compares to the millions of dollars the industry generates every year. Overall, tourism is Nepal's second largest source of foreign exchange, bringing in around $360 million per year. Climbing and trekking account for a significant portion of those earnings. The disparity between industry earnings and the modest wages paid to Sherpas has not gone unnoticed. Commenting on the tragic avalanche that killed sixteen Sherpas in 2014, Dhamey Tenzing Norgay, son of Tenzing, wrote: "The loss undercovers a growing divide between expedition members, who pay top dollar to reach the summit, and their highly skilled Sherpa guides, who are paid a relative pittance and too often are taken for granted."

Despite some minor concessions to Sherpas following the 2014 tragedy, the government has done little to improve the economic fortunes of Sherpas working on Everest. One of the key issues is the amount of compensation paid to the families whose fathers or brothers or sons have died on the mountain. The impact of the 2014 tragedy on Sherpa families and communities was profound. It left sixteen widows and twenty-eight dependent children behind. Following the tragedy, the government raised the life-insurance policies for climbing Sherpas from $10,000 to $15,000. Even so, this hardly compensates for the loss of a family's breadwinner. To make up for the financial deficiency, foreign climbers periodically organize fundraisers for surviving families. Expedition operators, who are required to purchase life-insurance policies for their employees, could help address this problem as well. For a mere $200 per worker, operators could voluntarily increase the insurance policy to $20,000. Regarding a Sherpa relief fund—something that has been discussed in the past—the government continually refuses to allocate any of its royalties for such a purpose. On the issue of wages, there still is no minimum wage for Sherpas working in the expedition industry.

Many changes have been proposed over the years that would make climbing Everest safer, especially for Sherpas who bear most of the risk. For starters, the government could limit the number of permits it issues per year to address the problem of overcrowding. Of course, this would limit the amount of royalties it receives, something it has demonstrated it is unwilling to do. To recoup any losses incurred by limiting the number of permits, the government could always raise its permit fee, although this might make Everest increasingly unavailable for all but the wealthiest clients. Another way to prevent overcrowding on the mountain is to limit the size of climbing teams. This could reduce the number and size of traffic jams on the mountain. It has even been suggested that the guide-to-client ratio be reduced to one-to-one, a situation where each client would have his or her own personal guide. In that scenario, client and guide could always be roped together.

One attractive option in addressing the problem of overcrowding is to cut down on the number of inexperienced climbers. This could be achieved by requiring anyone interested in climbing Everest to first scale a mountain in Nepal of, say, 23,000 feet or more. A big problem with inexperienced climbers is that no one knows how their bodies will perform at high elevations. If enforced properly, this requirement could remove a lot of that uncertainty, and maybe even increase tourist revenue in the country. Although Everest climbers are currently required to have experience on another peak of at least 6,000 meters, the regulation is not strictly enforced.

Expedition operators have recently become more vocal about the dangers faced by Sherpas who repeatedly must pass through the Ice Fall, convincing the government to temporarily allow helicopters to transport gear directly from Base Camp to Camp II. It has also been proposed that Camp II become far less luxurious so that Sherpas have less gear to haul up and down the mountain. Another way to increase safety for Sherpas is to limit the weight of their loads, thereby increasing their chances of survival in an avalanche.

Perhaps the most effective way to reduce risk on Everest is to ban bottled oxygen except in cases of medical emergencies. As unrealistic as this option may seem, it certainly would reduce the number of marginally competent climbers on the mountain, who likely wouldn't attempt the ascent in the first place. The use of bottled oxygen on Everest has been controversial ever since the British introduced an early form of it in 1921, prompting some Sherpas to label it "English Air." Without supplemental oxygen, especially in "the death zone" above 8,000 meters, the human body becomes particularly susceptible to a range of physical disorders including hypothermia, frostbite, and both cerebral and pulmonary edema. Of the nearly 5,000 people who have summitted Everest, only 208 have done so without supplemental oxygen. Banning bottled oxygen would also help reduce the amount of rubbish on the mountain.

Without question, the Everest industry has suffered from the government's lack of vision and leadership. A big part of the problem lies in its instability, demonstrated by the fact that Nepal has had six different prime ministers since democratic reforms were instituted in 2008. Ang Tshering describes the situation this way: "The ministers and secretaries are often changing, and before they understand something they've already changed," he said. "Every time a minister tries to do something, that minister changes. And a minister who knows nothing about tourism comes. This is one of the most difficult parts of life here." Peedom echoes this sentiment: "You can spend a year lobbying [government officials], and three weeks later they're out of a job. There's a lot of turmoil and turnover in that job."

Compounding the situation is the fact that the two nations that control access to the peak—Nepal and Tibet—are both desperately poor. The governments of both countries have a vested interest in issuing as many climbing permits as the market will support, and both are reluctant to enact any policies that limit their revenues. Be that as it may, there is mounting pressure in the climbing community for more meaningful government action.

Certainly, the Nepal government and expedition operators need to do more to solve the problems that plague the Everest industry. But it is also incumbent upon clients, the expedition members, to understand the ethics of climbing Everest, and their role in how the industry is conducted. After all, it is the money from clients that drives the entire industry. This responsibility is particularly important when it comes to Sherpa safety and compensation. Anyone looking to climb Everest through a commercial operator needs to research the record and profile of the operator, especially as it relates to the safety and compensation of its workers. This includes the porters.

Not all Nepalese porters are Sherpas; many are from poor families in the lowlands or belong to other ethnic groups such as the Tamang, Magars, or Rai. Some of these workers may not be prepared to be high-elevation porters because they are unaccustomed to the altitude, not outfitted properly, or lacking in education and experience. Consequently, they run the risk of hypothermia, frostbite, and elevation sickness. I myself have seen porters dying on the side of the trail, others taken down from the mountain dead. Trekking companies, as well as trekkers themselves, need to take more responsibility for the welfare of their porters. Too often, companies just want to maximize profit, disregarding the health and safety of their workers. This is one of the biggest problems in the trekking industry today. The Nepal government is particularly negligent when it comes to looking out for porters. Any trekker who goes into the Himalayas ought to be aware enough to check on the treatment and equipment of their porters.

Meanwhile, climbing Everest has only become more popular. The allure of summiting the world's tallest mountain is as strong as ever, attracting people from around the globe. Based on current trends, we should expect Everest to become more crowded and more expensive to climb. We should also anticipate that an average of eight people will lose their lives every year. Climbing Everest has always been an extremely dangerous undertaking and doubtless always will be. Few of the clients on the peak truly appreciate the gravity of the risks they face—the thinnest of margins by which human life is sustained above 25,000 feet. The combination of poor government oversight, inexperienced climbers, and subpar expedition operators only contributes to the danger.

Overall, I believe people need to have a greater respect for the mountain and a deeper appreciation of it as a sacred place. Perhaps the best way for Westerners to cultivate this appreciation is through an understanding of Sherpa traditions and spirituality. In the words of Pem Pem Tshering: "Jomolungma is mother goddess of the earth—you must respect her as a sanctity. She is a sanctity." And this from Tenzing's son, Jamling Tenzing Norgay: "It's a holy place....Westerners approach it as a physical challenge—push limits to see how close you can get to death, but Sherpas have thousands-year-old stories of mountains, history which Westerners have no idea about. Some people adapt and learn and respect it, some people don't."

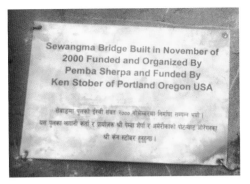

M-17 helicopter lands in Sengma with supplies for the bridge

Sengma Bridge dedication

Sengma Suspension Bridge, completed in 2000

The original hydro-electric station in Sengma

*Counting money for
earthquake victims*

Earthquake damage to a house in Khumbu

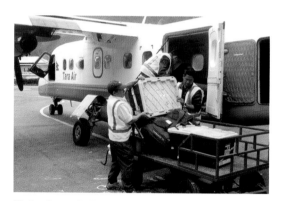

*Unloading relief supplies for earthquake
victims at Lukla airport*

*Hauling relief supplies
for earthquake victims*

Children studying in a tent after the earthquake

The new hydro station in Sengma

*Pipeline for the new hydro
station in Sengma*

*Hauling water pipe
to Sengma*

Earthquake victims in Chhourikharka, June 2015

Distributing money to earthquake victims, Chhourikharka

Sherpa Chai

CHAPTER SEVENTEEN
Earthquake

Just before noon on April 25, 2015, Nepal was hit by a catastrophic earthquake of 7.8 magnitude. With its epicenter located forty-eight miles northwest of Kathmandu, the quake was felt throughout central and eastern Nepal, as well as in parts of India, Bangladesh, Tibet, and Bhutan. Two large aftershocks, registering 6.6 and 6.7 magnitude, occurred within an hour of the main quake. These were followed by several dozen smaller aftershocks in the days ahead. The main quake, which has come to be known as the Ghorka earthquake, was triggered by a sudden release of built-up stress along the major

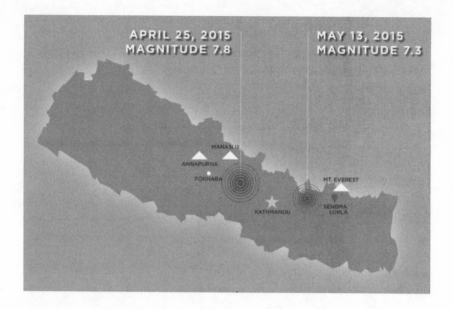

fault-line where the Indian Plate is slowly sliding under the Eurasian Plate. Nepal lies completely within the collision zone between the Indian subcontinent and Eurasia.

The effects of the quake were devastating. Nearly 9,000 people died and another 22,000 were injured. Up to four million people were left homeless, as entire villages were destroyed. On May 12, two-and-a-half weeks after the initial quake, an aftershock measuring 7.3 magnitude shook the country again. This epicenter was located forty-seven miles east-northeast of Kathmandu near the Chinese border. More than 100 people were killed following the aftershock, and another 1,900 were injured. In the end, total damage from the 2015 earthquake in Nepal was estimated to be $9 billion, an amount equivalent to nearly half the nation's nominal GDP.

The Ghorka quake on April 25th triggered a number of avalanches in the area of Mount Everest, including one on the nearby peak of Pumori that swept through South Base Camp. Nineteen bodies were recovered from the avalanche, making it the deadliest day on the mountain, breaking the record of sixteen set just the year before. The following day, as rescuers were trying to repair the route through the Icefall, another aftershock struck, taking out most of the ladders and killing another three workers. In all, twenty-four people were killed on Everest as a result of avalanches caused by the earthquake, at least thirteen of whom were Sherpas. Routes through the Icefall were closed for the season, making 2015 the first time in forty-one years that no one reached the summit of the mountain.

Almost immediately, I started receiving calls from family members in Nepal asking for help. I soon learned that my cousin Dawa, whom I had known since childhood, had died while working at Base Camp. He left a widow and an infant son in

Chhourikharka. Their house was completely demolished in the earthquake. In fact, nearly everyone I knew in Nepal had their houses destroyed or damaged. The scale of the catastrophe was overwhelming. With my own money, I could maybe help four or five families rebuild their homes, but the devastation that occurred required a relief effort that would have to be massive in scale. Not only that, time was of the essence. People needed assistance immediately. Having no experience in anything like this, I realized I needed to consult with someone for advice. I decided to contact my friends at the Colorado Mountain Club.

CMC went to work right away, calling a meeting the very next day. As a nonprofit organization, CMC had experience in raising money. They advised me on how to lead a fundraising campaign, helping me to set up a webpage where people could donate money to the relief effort. They hosted a dinner and auction that raised $42,000. In addition, we held public events in Boulder, Denver, Golden, and Lyons, where I presented a slide show and spoke about the humanitarian crisis in Nepal. At each event, I donated food from the restaurant.

In just a few months time, we raised $110,000. We also received donations from North Face, Mountain Hardware, Kelty, and Osprey in the way of clothes, sleeping bags, and tents. Mc-Guckin Hardware in Boulder provided 150 tarps that could be used for temporary living arrangements. I wired the $110,000 to my brother's account in Nepal so that we could quickly distribute the money to people in need. Wary of the government's reputation for corruption and ineptitude, I booked a flight to Nepal so I could oversee delivery of the money myself. A friend of mine, Greg Greenstreet, offered to go with me. We each paid our own air fare, guaranteeing that all the donated money would go directly to people who needed it most. We brought $65,000 worth of clothes, tents, tarps, and sleeping bags with us on the flight, all packed into forty-eight duffel bags. United Airlines graciously waived the baggage fee, saving us $15,000. I was truly grateful for the outpouring of generosity from everyone involved.

Greg and I flew to Nepal in June with all the gear. When we landed in Kathmandu, customs officials stopped us at the airport and seized our supplies. Based on what I knew about Nepal's corrupt bureaucracy, this didn't come as a complete surprise. Nevertheless, it was extremely frustrating. Mariko and I had spent two weeks packing all the gear, I'd transported it to

Relief supplies for earthquake victims

the other side of the planet, and now I couldn't get it the final fifty feet to where I could distribute it to people in dire need.

I soon discovered that there was a whole warehouse filled with food and gear intended for earthquake victims—relief supplies that customs agents had seized and were not releasing. Meanwhile, people were dying in the mountains every day. This was one of the most disappointing moments of my life. Frustrated and angry, I confronted the airport officials. I wanted to grab the Customs Chief by the scruff of the neck and throw him against the wall.

Greg and I spent three days in Kathmandu, trying to get the forty-eight duffel bags released. Finally, we gave up and departed for Chhourikharka where we had arranged to distribute the money. After exchanging the $110,000 into Nepali currency, the cash we carried weighed 18 kilos. When we arrived in Chhourikharka and informed everyone about the gear that had been confiscated in Kathmandu, people became irate to the point of wanting to riot. I advised them instead to pressure the government through political channels. Based on past experience, I knew the best way to proceed was to notify a regional political leader, who could then apply pressure on the government in Kathmandu. I was acutely aware of the fact that, in Nepal, international aid doesn't always end up in the hands of the people who need it. This is why I had flown there in the first place.

Before coming to Nepal, I had gone through a lengthy process of determining which groups were most in need. Because of its low status in the caste system, the Bishukarma tribe has historically been discriminated against and oppressed. Thus, we gave priority to people from this group who'd been most affected by the earthquake. At the school in Chhourikharka, I gave a speech in which I emphasized the importance of working cooperatively. I implored everyone to come together, all families and villages, and not discriminate against anyone on the basis

Hauling relief supplies from Lukla to Chhourikharka

of caste or political affiliation. This was not the time to allow old grievances or biases to intervene.

I spent two weeks in Nepal, seeing that the aid was fairly and effectively distributed. I am happy to report that every dollar which was raised in the fundraising campaign went directly to people who needed it. With the money that was donated, we helped 282 families rebuild their homes. In addition, we helped rebuild two monasteries, one temple, and the bridge in Phakding across the Dudh Koshi.

After months of delay, the duffel bags were finally released. As I anticipated, a political leader from Khumbu contacted the district senator, who then applied pressure on customs officials.

Once I learned that our gear was to be released, I returned to Nepal to help distribute it.

The corruption and greed of government officials in Kathmandu remains a serious national problem. In April of 2017, Nepal's National Reconstruction Authority reported that only five percent of the 824,000 houses destroyed in the earthquake had been rebuilt, and only twelve percent of the reconstruction money had been distributed. Two years after the earthquake, 800,000 families still were without their homes. To make matters worse, financial assistance was denied to people who did not own property, exacerbating the social divide that continues to plague the country.

CHAPTER EIGHTEEN
Sherpa Tea

When confronted with a disaster as large and catastrophic as the 2015 earthquake, it can be difficult to know how to help. Because I had friends and family in Khumbu, my first concern was for the people living there who had been impacted the most. The urgency of the situation demanded immediate action, but the destruction was so overwhelming that it was impossible to respond to every request for help. Among the many requests I received, my friends in Sengma asked if I could restore the hydropower station which we had built eight years earlier. Like many structures, the station had been destroyed in the earthquake. At the time, I was preoccupied with helping people rebuild their homes. It was not until I returned to the U.S. that I had time to think about the project.

A year prior to the earthquake, I'd come up with the idea of marketing a line of chai. Popular with customers, the chai we served at the restaurant was made from the same recipe that my mother used when I was a child. In fact, it was the same tea that she gave me every morning before I started my long walk to school. When I researched the market for bottled tea, I was surprised to find there were only a few products out there, and none were authentic in terms of the chai traditionally brewed in Nepal, India, or Tibet. After registering the product, gaining FDA certification, and designing a label, we launched Sherpa Tea.

It was in the process of promoting Sherpa Tea that I happened to meet Heather Bulk. I was offering free samples at McGuckin Hardware when she approached me about helping victims of the earthquake. She'd recently established a non-profit organization designed to achieve this very goal. When she asked if I had any advice about what she could do, I answered that there were many ways to help. I told her that if she were interested, I would work with her on a campaign to raise funds to rebuild the hydro facility in Sengma. In a relatively short period of time, we were able to raise $37,000.

Once the funding was in place, I contacted my brother Chhongba in Kathmandu, who agreed to oversee the project. With the money that Heather had raised, we now had an opportunity to build a permanent, continuously operating facility. But it would not be easy. The normal challenges of transporting materials to Khumbu and installing the facility in Sengma were complicated by the devastation caused by the earthquake. Road closures and higher transportation costs made the task even more difficult.

Not to be discouraged, Chhongba arranged to transport the materials by bus from Kathmandu to Paphlu. From there, they were flown by helicopter to Lukla where they were carried the final few miles on foot to Sengma. The project was completed in 2016. Today, the facility supplies Sengma and other outlying areas with regular and continuous electricity. What's more, the telephone company that provides service to Khumbu built its satellite tower in Sengma to take advantage of the power generated at the facility. Today, the entire Khumbu region enjoys high-speed internet service.

In the four years since we launched Sherpa Tea, sales have increased dramatically with an annual growth rate of 200 percent. In the first year, our total sales came to $3,000 for the entire year. Currently, our sales are at $90,000 *per month*. Our product is available in four states at such major chains as Whole Foods, Sprouts, National Grocer, and Kroger. We've recently contracted with United Natural Foods, Inc. (UNFI), one of the largest distributors in the world. With this kind of growth potential, I'm already looking to the future. My goal is to buy land in Nepal to grow tea for the company. To run the plantation, I want to hire Nepalese women who have been victimized by the sex trade.

It is often the case that natural disasters in poor nations create social problems that can take years, if not decades, to overcome. Among the many social crises that befell Nepal in the wake of the earthquake, human traffickers descended on the country to prey upon girls and women, especially those from poor communities who had lost their homes. Single women in particular had very little access to relief during this time. Human traffickers targeted the women in order to supply the brothels of South Asia. Today, even if they've been fortunate to escape the sex trade and return home, Nepali girls and women are not always welcome back in the communities where they were raised because of what's happened to them. Many are ostracized.

This is an injustice that needs to be rectified. As a businessman, I see an opportunity to help these women by providing them with a safe and supportive place to live and start a career. Sometimes it's not enough to rescue people from their tragic circumstances. It may also be necessary to provide economic opportunities so they can support themselves and recover a measure of self-esteem. My plan is to establish a program whereby I extend small loans to these women in order to help them start their own tea farms. Sherpa Tea would then buy their product, providing them with a reliable market to sell their tea. In the process of operating their farms, they would learn valuable business skills that they could utilize throughout their lives.

CHAPTER NINETEEN
A New Generation

Sherpa people have traveled a long road since their exodus from Tibet centuries ago. Living in relative isolation in Solokhumbu, a remote part of the world closed to foreigners, early Sherpas developed a unique culture based on Buddhist principles and an agrarian way of life. That all began to change in the 20th Century when British climbing teams hired Sherpas to support mountain expeditions in the Himalaya. As the climbing industry developed and Nepal opened its borders to outsiders, Sherpas distinguished themselves as exceptional mountaineers and gained a reputation worldwide as legendary dwellers of the high Himalaya. Today, people come to Khumbu from all corners of the globe to climb mountains, enjoy trekking, and experience Sherpa culture. The tourist trade has provided Sherpa people with economic opportunities and access to the outside world, improving their standard of living in Khumbu and beyond.

In 1960, when Sirdar Urkien told Hillary that Sherpa children lacked education, saying that "our children have eyes but they cannot see," he identified the key element that would transform Sherpa society into what it is today. In the sixty years since that conversation around the campfire, a younger Sherpa generation has emerged that is different even from my own. When I was growing up, virtually no one in Khumbu attended high school. Today, perhaps 80 percent of Sherpa children earn a high school diploma. Many leave home at age five to attend boarding school in Kathmandu where they continue their education until graduating from high school, learning English and preparing themselves for the global economy. At that point, they may pursue opportunities anywhere in the world, turning their backs on the climbing industry that made many of their parents relatively prosperous. I have a Sherpa friend who operates a lodge in Khumbu. He has five children who are living in different parts of the world including Australia, New York, Belgium, and Korea.

Many Sherpa parents, especially those who have benefited financially from the tourist business, feel an obligation to educate their children in Western ways to improve their chances of making a good living. Boarding school can be quite rigorous, and children often feel pressured to please their parents. Still, many families prefer the opportunities provided by formal education to any benefits there may be from working in the climbing industry. Sherpas are all too familiar with the risks inherent in mountaineering. To quote Jamling Tenzing Norgay: "My father said he climbed so we wouldn't have to. He wanted to give us the best education so we could continue our lives in some other career besides climbing because climbing is dangerous."

There are other factors besides education that have influenced the way this younger generation views the world. Many Sherpas today have grown up with computers and the internet. Like young people all over the world, they have cell phones and participate in social media. They are more sophisticated than what Westerners might presume, especially those who choose to view Sherpas through the lens of faithful servants, an idealized image that gained traction after Tenzing's ascent of Everest in 1953.

As for young Sherpas who decide to go into the climbing industry, many have asserted themselves in ways that haven't been seen before. No longer content to play a servile role to Western climbers and operators, this younger generation is more aggressive in taking control of the industry itself. They've seen how Western climbers get the credit for climbing Everest, when they know full well that it wouldn't have been possible without the support of Sherpas. As climbers and guides, they view themselves as equals to Westerners and want to be acknowledged as such. They want to be recognized and given credit for what they have done.

The emergence of a more assertive younger generation was evident in 2012 when Sherpa climbers moved to close the climbing season on Mount Manaslu after an avalanche killed eleven people. It was on display again in 2014 when a group of expedition workers crafted a list of demands at Base Camp following the deadly avalanche on Everest, an event that exposed some of the generational differences among Sherpas. In the days following the tragedy, it seemed the authority of longtime *sirdars* on the mountain—men like Lakpa Rita, Ang Jangbu, Ang Dorjee, Lam Babu, and Phurba Tashi—had given way to a group of younger Sherpas who were not afraid to speak their minds and air their grievances.

One of the most notorious incidents on Everest in recent memory was the 2013 fistfight that took place at Camp II between three professional European climbers and a group of Sherpas. The Europeans had angered the Sherpas earlier in the day by climbing above them while the Sherpas were fixing rope on the Lhotse face. An argument took place in which one of the Europeans was heard to say "motherfucker," a profanity that should never to be uttered on the mountain. Later, an altercation ensued when a number of Sherpas confronted the Europeans at Camp II. Commenting on the fistfight, Phurba remarked that the foreigner was in the wrong, but that the Sherpas should not have lost their composure like they did. Lakpa Rita went further, wondering aloud if he wanted to climb Everest anymore in the wake of what happened.

Any difference between generations shouldn't come as

a complete surprise, not when you consider the different circumstances in which they've lived. Unlike their parents, most younger Sherpas have received a formal education and grown up with the internet. Many have traveled overseas. What's more, this younger generation came of age in a brutal Civil War stemming from the historic rise of democracy in their country.

It's also important to recognize the transition that's taking place in the industry itself. Sherpas are not just porters anymore. If older Sherpas have made a good career of working for Western operators, many younger Sherpas are training to become international mountain guides by earning their IFMGA certifications—a long and expensive process that qualifies a guide to work anywhere in the world at a higher wage. Many go on to work for local outfitters based in Kathmandu. This new group of Nepali outfitters consists mainly of Sherpas who seem intent on taking control of all phases of Everest expeditions.

The relationship with foreigners and outside influence has always been a complicated issue for Sherpa people. On the positive side, money generated from the tourist trade has brought extraordinary benefits in the form of schools, health care, infrastructure, and a higher standard of living. Many improvements have come by way of grants from international relief organizations as well. Sherpa families have benefited from greater access to the outside world and the opportunities it presents. I myself have taken advantage of opportunities in the United States and the standard of living they have provided for my family. Overall, I believe the changes that I've seen in my lifetime have been for the better.

Certainly, some of these changes have come at a cost. For instance, families have had to live apart in the pursuit of opportunities beyond Khumbu. This is especially true in the case of parents who send their young children to boarding school in Kathmandu for a better education. It has long been a dream of mine to see a boarding school built in Khumbu, so that Sherpa children can receive an excellent education without having to be separated from their families for extended periods of time. There are other ways families become separated. Parents sometimes travel abroad for better paying jobs while their children remain in Nepal. This is the case with a couple who works at my restaurant in Boulder. To maintain close ties, a hallmark of Sherpa culture, families rely on telephones and social media to stay connected.

Another big concern is the loss of traditional culture. With so many young people leaving home for Kathmandu and elsewhere, coupled with the influx of foreign visitors to Khumbu, Sherpas today are not as invested in traditional culture as earlier generations were. While older Sherpas continue to dress in traditional clothing, younger people wear t-shirts bearing the names of Western sports teams and rock bands. Many have seen the latest American movies and played the latest video games. As thoroughly assimilated into American culture as I am, I too worry that younger Sherpas are losing aspects of traditional culture, such as work ethic, respect for others, and the Sherpa language itself. Younger Sherpas are no longer speaking their native language. Now when I am in Khumbu, I find myself speaking Nepali with younger Sherpas. Like many indigenous languages throughout the world, it could be that the Sherpa language is destined for extinction.

Another cause for concern is the sheer number of outsiders presently living in Khumbu. With so many younger Sherpas choosing careers outside the climbing industry, Nepalis from other ethnic groups come to Khumbu to take advantage of the porter jobs. American and European climbers continue to request Sherpas for their expeditions, but support positions are increasingly being filled by Nepalis who are not Sherpas. The presence of outsiders living and working in Khumbu is worrisome for Sherpas who are concerned about preserving their traditional culture. The fact that so many outsiders live in the valley now has even created some animosity.

A big challenge facing Sherpas today is how to engage globalization without losing their culture and traditions. Frankly, I'm not sure this is possible. For most of human history, the experience of people was limited to their immediate surroundings in terms of language, customs, religion, food, music, and art. Now, thanks to television, the internet, air travel, and other features of modern life, people are free to experience and enjoy other cultures. No longer restricted by the constraints imposed on them by their native culture, they are free to find their place in the global village.

As important as it may be to preserve traditional culture, it is also important to recognize that some aspects of it may not be worth saving. Arranged marriages are a good example.

Although arranged marriages still occur in Sherpa society, this tradition has mostly fallen by the wayside. The caste system is another tradition in Nepal that is not worth preserving. Nepal is home to many different ethnic groups, and some of these groups are discriminated against and treated badly. Inherited from India, the caste system is a form of racism that even Sherpas participate in from time to time. I remember once as a little boy bringing a friend home, only to have my mother prevent him from entering the house because he was a member of an inferior caste. I knew right away this was wrong. After years of traveling the world and experiencing different cultures, my feelings on this issue have only grown stronger.

Sherpas can often feel as though they are caught between worlds. This is particularly true for those of us who were raised in a traditional way, but now find ourselves living abroad. While in the United States, I am always aware of my Sherpa heritage. By the same token, when I return to Khumbu, the place where I was born and raised, I am reminded of how much life in the U.S. has influenced me. Always there is this difference. Oftentimes I find myself trying to reconcile this duality and bridge the two worlds. I'd like to think that there is a happy medium, a balance that brings together the best of both worlds.

I have a friend named Dendi who lives near Ghat. Retired now from the tourist industry, he is old enough to remember when there was no electricity in Khumbu and kerosene lamps were first introduced for lighting. He came of age at a time when the greater valley, from Lukla clear to Mount Everest, was for all intents and purposes a Sherpa kingdom. Today, he lives with his wife Ami in a new house that was built after his former home was destroyed in the earthquake. Because of the threat of Glacial Lake Outburst Floods (GLOFs)—a threat that has increased in recent years due to global warming—they have built their new house on a hillside away from the river.

Like many Sherpas, Dendi and Ami keep scrolls of Buddhist prayers rolled up in their wooden cabinets. Ami wears a *togkok*, the traditional long-sleeved dress worn by Sherpa women. Over the dress, she wears a striped apron called a *metil*, held in place by a large, embossed silver buckle known as a *kyetis*. Every morning she makes her *yonchap*, pouring water into seven copper bowls before placing them in a line from left to right on her shrine. She purifies their home, inside and out, with an offering of incense created by swinging a brazier filled with burning juniper.

Meanwhile, their house is powered by solar panels and a small hydro-generator situated along a nearby stream. They own a television that brings in a station from Kathmandu by way of a satellite dish. They have satellite phones and WiFi. There is a guest bedroom at the back of the house that trekkers can rent by the night. Outside in greenhouses, they grow an array of fruits and vegetables: beans, tomatoes, carrots, peas, chard, arugula, kale, bok choy, hops, garlic, cauliflower, cabbage, corn, buckwheat and barley. Apples and plums, pears and peaches. They have a *nak* that provides them with milk and cheese. The house has gravity-fed running water, and a solar hot-water tank on the roof. Rocks have been moved aside and piled into low walls along the perimeter of the property. Other rocks are situated in the hillside above the house, where for centuries they have served as steps along the path to Ghat.

The couple has two sons, one who is a scientist in Portugal, and another who has entered a local monastery. Although Dendi is concerned about Sherpas losing their traditional culture, he understands that no one is going to stand in the way of young people pursuing careers abroad or embracing a Western way of life. Likewise, no one is going to deny Sherpas living in Khumbu the opportunity to improve their lives through modern technology. There is still poverty in the region that needs to be addressed through education, economic opportunity, modern medicine, and better infrastructure.

At the same time, life in the valley has a lot to offer. Khumbu is recognized around the world as one of the most beautiful places on earth, a place considered sacred by the Sherpas who live there. The traditional culture offers a way of life where spirituality is intertwined with everyday living, a way of life grounded in nature and bound together through ritual and ceremony. It is a place that values close family ties, where friends walk long distances to visit over a cup of tea. As demanding as life can be in Khumbu, it offers a valuable model of how to live well in a place.

CHAPTER TWENTY
Khumbu Today

Following the 1952 Cho Oyu reconnaissance expedition, Hillary and other members of his team journeyed to the east of Everest where they came upon the Barun valley. Hillary wrote about the experience in *View from the Summit*:

> "The valley floor was covered by some square miles of flowering crimson azaleas—a truly magnificent sight.... The monsoon rain had transformed the landscape, and myriads of tiny blossoms of every color were bursting through the arid soil.... We were now in a world of rain, hundreds of waterfalls drifted gracefully down the mighty rock bluffs

and the heavy clouds would split for a moment
to reveal some startling summit before closing in
again with torrential rain. I felt it was the most
beautiful valley I had ever seen and I felt sure I
would return to enjoy its flowers and sparkling
streams and soaring peaks. As we sheltered under
an overhanging rock one of our senior and highly
respected Sherpas told us a story. Dawa Tenzing
had never been in the Barun valley before, but
Sherpa mythology told of its existence. The valley
contained an invisible village—a Shangri-La—
where the gods lived and holy men came to die.
It was a place of great beauty, as we had seen,
and people lived there forever."

In the years since, Khumbu has become a popular destination for climbers and trekkers from all over the globe. Today,
an average of more than 50,000 tourists visit the region annually. On top of that, thousands of porters and workers from
elsewhere in Nepal travel to Khumbu to carry loads or work in
the fields. To accommodate the traffic of visitors, Khumbu has
undergone significant development in the form of new lodges and teahouses, as the economy becomes increasingly reliant
on the tourist trade. While tourism has improved the lives of

Sherpas overall, it has come with a price. The influx of outsiders not only poses a threat to traditional culture, but it has created a number of environmental problems, especially deforestation and water pollution.

In the centuries that people have lived in Khumbu, forests have been converted to pastureland for yaks and other livestock. As the trekking industry grew in popularity beginning in the 1960s, the pressure on forests became even greater as more lumber was required for new construction and more firewood was needed for cooking and heating. But this trend may be changing. Today, valley residents are cooking less with firewood and more with propane and electricity. As a result, the forests in Khumbu, which were visibly in decline by the 1980s, are showing signs of recovery. Livestock grazing is down as well, and in some places, trees have reclaimed land that had once been used as pasture.

The recovery of forests in Khumbu did not happen by accident. Due largely to the leadership of Mingma Norbu Sherpa, warden of Sagamartha National Park, local communities went to work on forest protection projects. At the same time, a Unesco project employed local labor to build a micro-hydroelectric plant on a hillside below Namche, utilizing water from a spring in the middle of town. These two initiatives set the stage for a healthier, more sustainable future in Khumbu.

Until recently, most Sherpas burned firewood in clay stoves known as *chulos*. This inefficient method was made worse by the fact that, without proper chimneys, smoke filled the insides of homes and caused health problems, especially among children. When steel stoves were introduced in the late 1990s and early 2000s, Khumbu residents began to burn yak dung for heating. Propane gas tanks were then introduced, offering a cleaner and cheaper fuel source for cooking. Meanwhile, the increase in small hydroelectric capacity provided more energy for lighting and household appliances. In recent years, the valley has seen a greater use of solar energy.

Other environmental problems, however, appear to be getting worse. For instance, garbage and human waste continue to accumulate not only on Mount Everest but throughout Sagamartha National Park. For decades, climbers have discarded empty gas and oxygen cylinders, damaged equipment, plastic wrappers, cans, and other trash on the mountain and surrounding areas. By the 1990s, the route to Everest had become so littered with waste that it was referred to as the "Kleenex trail." In response, climbers, outfitters, and Sherpas initiated efforts to remove trash from the mountain. Today, organizations like the Everest Summiteers Association, Nepal Mountaineering Association, and Sagamartha Pollution Control Committee (SPCC) work to clean up not only Everest but the entire Park. Even the central government has become involved, instituting regulations which require climbing teams to return with a minimum amount of trash. But the problems persist. The SPCC's resources are limited, and the government's waste-management rules aren't well enforced.

The situation on Everest is particularly troubling, not only because of what many cite as the negligent habits of inexperienced climbers, but also because the mountain's glaciers are melting and exposing litter that's been buried for decades. Adding to the problem is the challenge of where to put the garbage once it is removed from the mountain. The trash problem off the mountain is every bit as daunting as the one on it. Dozens of landfills already exist near villages and lodges throughout the National Park.

In April 2019, a major clean-up operation was launched on

Everest as part of a coordinated effort involving Nepal's tourism department, local government officials, and mountaineering groups. The operation was scheduled to last forty-five days with the overall goal of removing eleven tons of garbage from the mountain, roughly a third of the trash believed to be there. Retreating glaciers not only have exposed buried garbage, but dead bodies as well. In the first two weeks of the operation alone, four corpses were recovered at Base Camp.

Perhaps most worrisome of all is the human waste that has been accumulating on the mountain for decades, especially near the four camps where every year climbers spend weeks acclimatizing to the altitude. In the absence of toilets, climbers have typically dug holes in the snow, or straddled small crevasses. Frozen fecal matter does not degrade quickly, and, if not disposed of properly, can continue to pose a risk of contaminating the water supply system for years to come. In the past, human waste has been bagged up and deposited in riverbeds where monsoon rains wash it downstream.

Sanitation has long been a concern in Khumbu, as it has throughout Nepal. According to a 2001 report issued by the Massachusetts Institute of Technology, 44,000 children under the age of five die annually in Nepal due to water-borne diseases. Perhaps one in six Sherpa children dies before the age of five, much of that traced to poor sanitation. Contaminated drinking water in Khumbu is caused by a combination of factors: the lack of proper waterworks, the absence of a sewage system, and the overwhelming number of tourists who visit the valley. For decades, solid waste has accumulated along mountain trails, valleys, and glaciers, contributing to fecal contamination of fresh water sources. Animal waste, primarily from yaks and other livestock, adds to the problem.

Unlike the four higher camps, Base Camp is equipped with toilet tents and drums to collect human waste. Once filled, the drums are taken to a frozen lake bed near Gorak Shep, a small village located at 17,000 feet elevation. Each year, Sherpa specialists carry and deposit more than twenty-five tons of human waste into the lake bed. But because of persistent freezing temperatures, the waste doesn't naturally degrade. Instead, it continues to accumulate, posing a threat of leaking into a nearby river.

Garry Porter, a retired mountaineer and engineer from the state of Washington, recently founded the Mount Everest

Biogas Project, along with fellow climber Dan Mazur. The project aims to clean up Gorak Shep by processing the human waste in an anaerobic digester system designed to break down the waste into methane gas and a pathogen-reduced effluent. The methane can then be used for cooking and lighting, while the effluent could potentially be used as fertilizer for crops. In order for the process to work, the digester needs to be kept at a consistently warm temperature so that bacteria can effectively feed upon the organic waste. To accomplish this, the Project will utilize a solar panel array to transmit heat into the digester. The Project is estimated to cost a half million dollars. Much of that money is needed simply to transport the equipment to Gorak Shep. Once they've raised the funds through donations, they have an agreement with the SPCC to begin construction. Ultimately, operation of the facility will be turned over to the SPCC.

Having experienced Everest as a climber, Porter has this to say about the mountain: "I think you need to earn Everest. I owe something. It's not my mountain. I'm just there. And I should leave it … as clean as I found it."

There are other environmental threats to Khumbu. Two

large hydroelectric projects, reportedly of 80 megawatts and 200 megawatts, have been proposed on the Dudh Kosi between Ghat and Djorsaale. Khumbu is already 90 percent electrified and would benefit very little from these facilities, if at all. Instead, the electricity generated by the projects would be exported to the Nepal electrical grid as well as to India. Both diversion-and-tunnel systems, if built, would have an enormous impact on the already fragile ecology of Khumbu.

The environmental challenges in Khumbu are compounded by a number of factors that make solving the problems all the more difficult: the nation's poverty, the region's remoteness and inaccessibility, and a tourist trade that continues to grow. There is no waste treatment facility in Khumbu, and no comprehensive recycling program. Because Everest is a major source of fresh water in Asia, contamination of the water system could potentially have far-reaching consequences.

The Khumbu region will never again be the "Shangri-La" that Hillary and other Western visitors imagined it was back in the fifties and sixties. The burgeoning tourist industry has seen to that, an industry that began with visitors such as Hillary intent on climbing Mount Everest. As much as Sherpas are concerned about the influx of tourists and its impact on the environment and traditional culture, they are also aware of the benefits that tourism has brought in the way of economic opportunities, education, and health care. For Sherpas, it is a balancing act. "Khumbu" is the Sherpa word for "sanctuary." Preserving that sense of sanctuary represents a major challenge going forward.

CHAPTER TWENTY-ONE

A Sherpa's Story

I see my life as a journey of experiences both good and bad, with lessons learned along the way. Born into poverty in the Himalayas of Nepal, I've become a successful American businessman and philanthropist. I've traveled widely and met people from all over the world, filtering all my experiences from a perspective that is both Sherpa and American. Within the Sherpa world itself, I am old enough to have grown up in the traditional culture, but young enough to have been part of many remarkable changes. There are valuable lessons to be learned from all experiences. I have come to realize that as much as Sherpas benefit from opportunities outside of Nepal, a Sherpa perspective has a lot to offer the rest of the world.

I am grateful for the opportunities that I have found in the U.S., and I feel blessed to be in a position where I can help so many people, especially my family and friends in Khumbu. I have witnessed many improvements in my native country over the years in terms of health care, education, infrastructure, and economic opportunity. In fact, great strides are being made around the world in the fight against disease, poverty, and illiteracy. Much of this is due to the science, technology, and support provided by Western organizations. There is much to appreciate about the West beyond its generosity and economic opportunities: freedom of expression, cultural pluralism, democratic safeguards against tyranny and oppression. Western countries are not without their flaws, of course, but we should never take for granted the civil liberties that we enjoy in the West. If the citizenry has faith in its society, then the nation has hope. The country has strength and resilience. Despite all the problems and challenges we face in the world, I am hopeful about the future.

I believe the experiences of my childhood taught me survival skills that have served me well in life, instilling in me the values of hard work, resourcefulness, perseverance, and patience. Despite the hardships of living in poverty, I cherish the fond memories of my early years—growing up with my brothers and sisters, living close to the land, being outside in a beautiful place. As difficult as it was, ours was a life of simplicity, free of complication. I am reminded of how different my childhood was from those of my American friends. My parents never went to school. I didn't even see a book until I was seven or eight. The way I look at it, I received a different kind of education. My American friends might know more about mathematics or biology than I do, but if we needed to build a fire high in the Himalaya where there is no wood, I would be the only one who would know how to do that.

My education was acquired through observation, awareness, and experience. Perceptual learning is self-regulated in the sense that modification occurs without the necessity of reaffirmation. In other words, it occurs in the immediacy of external stimuli, requiring a sense of awareness and the ability to identify and act upon the specific demands of a particular situation. I like to use the example of learning to fly an airplane—an often confusing and terrifying experience that involves a number of different skills: deciphering the instrument panel, understanding forces of physics, processing information, exercising good judgment. All of these skills are brought to bear on reading and responding to conditions that are constantly changing.

Of course, not all learning experiences in life are pleasant. In Nepal, I was introduced to bigotry and the caste system at an early age. The problem of racism is not confined to Nepal, obviously. Whether it reveals itself in a caste system, institutional racism, or ethnic cleansing, it is a global problem. After coming to the U.S. where I was immediately classified as a minority because of my appearance and ethnicity, I decided to study the issue in more detail. Through my reading, I came to understand that the concept of "race" is a fiction. In other words, there is no underlying genetic basis to support the notion that humans are divided into biologically distinct "races." Yes, there are different ethnic groups, but "ethnicity" refers strictly to cultural traits. Even though it may be a fiction, the concept of race has very real socioeconomic consequences. It is used as a tool of political and economic power to benefit some groups and marginalize others. On the positive side, as much as prejudice and bigotry are learned behaviors, they can be *unlearned* through education and scientific literacy.

Not long ago, I was at the airport in Vancouver, Canada on my way to a business meeting. The customs agent, a woman of Indo-Aryan ancestry I would guess, looked at my U.S. passport and noticed that Nepal was my birthplace. Then she said, "Nepal... Sherpa." At that point, she started asking me a whole line of questions about my history, citizenship, place of residence, and so on. Finally, when she asked about my occupation, I told her that I was the CEO of my own company, and that she should stamp my passport and let me go. She then became more polite and said that she was only doing her job. I respect that, but it was clear she had stereotyped me as a porter who could not be trusted. Of course, my experience doesn't compare with that of African-Americans or other ethnic groups around the world, whose lives may be threatened on a daily basis simply because of how they look. But this is all the more reason to confront the issue of racism head on. That it may be an uncomfortable topic of discussion is no excuse, especially in the climate we live in today.

Immigrants, or the children of immigrants, have founded

or co-founded such legendary American companies as Google, Facebook, and Apple. Lest we forget, Steve Job's father's name was Abdulfattah Jandali. As an immigrant myself, I know from personal experience the contributions immigrants make to the American economy and its culture. I am a businessman, a risk-taker, whose skills have been forged in the experience of poverty and immigration. I come with a certain hunger and perspective that, far from diminishing the greatness of America, add to it. To embrace my success is to embrace the genius of America. Born and raised a Sherpa, I bring a unique perspective to the American experience.

Despite growing up poor in Sengma, I ate a healthy diet of organic foods, free of chemical fertilizers, herbicides, or pesticides. There was very little sugar in our diet. Unlike the United States where obesity is an epidemic, you won't find overweight people in Khumbu. On the other hand, being thin is not the same as being healthy. It's common knowledge that a healthy diet and regular exercise are essential for good health and wellness. Both require a degree of discipline and commitment over the long run. I am able to enjoy a wide range of foods, in part because I have a high metabolism from so many years of climbing in the Himalaya and because I continue to stay active. Virtually every day, I make time for running or cycling or climbing. I've been living in the U.S. for nearly three decades, and I've never once been to the hospital outside of regular check-ups.

At the same time, I pay $1,100 per month in health insurance for a family of three, with a very high deductible. This is more than the median household income worldwide. The health care system in the United States is expensive and wasteful. We spend twice as much money as many other countries while getting the same results. Although we may get better care in some areas, it is hard to make the case that the American health system provides a good return on the money that is spent. An emphasis on exercise, healthy food, and other preventive measures would go a long way in reducing cost and making sure health care is available for those who need it most.

In 2016, I opened a second restaurant in Boulder featuring a variety of Sherpa and Japanese cuisine. I named the restaurant "Fuji", after seeing Mount Fuji during one of my many visits to Japan with Mariko. While we were there, she introduced me to a popular lunchtime snack called *onigiri*. A longtime Japanese staple, onigiri consists of cooked rice wrapped in *nori*, or seaweed. The rice is lightly salted and can be flavored by any number of fillings: dressed tuna or salmon, mackerel, freshwater eel, cod roe, wild albacore, chicken, Japanese plum pickle and other vegetables. At Fuji, we serve onigiri with a cup of *miso shuri* soup that contains nori, onions, and tofu. As we do at "Sherpa's," we use fresh ingredients in all our food. Delicious, nutritious, and easy to prepare, a meal like this offers a healthy alternative to the standard lunch eaten by American children every day.

The problem of waste can be seen in other areas of American life. Our consumerist society generates an inordinate amount of waste in terms of resource use, land management, garbage and pollution. Approximately 40 percent of the food in the U.S. is thrown out or otherwise wasted. The depletion rate of aquifers and healthy topsoil is unsustainable. At some point, this comes down to accountability. What policy is it that is driving our system, and who among us are in positions of power to affect that policy?

In my travels around the world, I often find that people living in the Third World appear happier than Westerners, simply because Westerners have more complications in their lives. For many Americans, happiness is defined in terms of self-advancement and material wealth. But the satisfaction of achieving personal ambitions is fleeting—there will always be something more to achieve or acquire. When we feel stress and anxiety because our personal goals are not being met, this leads to a sense of not having enough time.

While it may be called "the root of all evil," money in and of itself is not the problem. In today's world, economic prosperity frees people from the physical hardships of poverty. For the billions of individuals living in poverty, a daily focus on money is certainly understandable. But for those who are blessed to have money and end up craving it as a measure of self-worth, this leads to endless confusion. It is indicative of an unhealthy attachment to money. In Tibetan, the word "attachment" is translated as *duchang*, which literally means "sticky desire." It signifies a desperate grasping at something, motivated by fear of separation from the object. One can see this in jealous relationships, for example, or an extreme need for social status. Such attachment often leads to avarice and envy. Getting beyond these snares is critical to life satisfaction.

I believe happiness depends upon good social relationships. I find this to be true for all people regardless of age, gender, ethnicity, or socioeconomic class. If we want to be happy, we should value and nurture the relationships we have with the people in our lives. By framing happiness in terms of the self, rather than something that occurs naturally through engaging the world, we place a premium on emotional independence and the expectation that contentment can only be found amid the intricacies and tripwires of our personalities. This approach is reflected not only in the way that many Americans talk about happiness, but in the ways they live their lives and spend their money.

Much of this stems from a cultural emphasis on individualism, bordering on narcissism. Messages in the media encourage people to be different, stand out from the crowd, be a star. A lot of this is commercially driven, designed to sell the idea that success is defined by material possessions. But it also plays into a broader cultural ethos. From an early age, children are reminded by parents and teachers of how special they are. Commencement speakers encourage young graduates to focus on themselves and follow their passions. While some of this encouragement appears benign, it fosters a worldview that begins and ends with the self. As Americans, we are encouraged to promote ourselves. Social media baits us into broadcasting a highlight reel of our lives to the point that experience becomes secondary to the image. Experience becomes just another form of consumerism, authenticated by the image uploaded on a smart phone.

One byproduct of extreme individualism is the absence of any real sense of social obligation. If we are taught to put ourselves first, this excuses us from any responsibility for the welfare of others. This attitude becomes a cultural norm, part of an overall mindset that informs our public policy and social systems. As a Nepali, I know all too well the social costs of a corrupt government. People must understand that we all are responsible for the well-being of ourselves, our communities, and the entire planet. Through courage and commitment, compassionate people can meet the challenges in their communities and in the world at large. It begins with vision. Vision is not a wish or hope that something will happen. It is a clear mental image of an end goal and what is required to achieve that goal. It is a clear idea of a future reality that depends upon work undertaken now.

People on the road to inner light do not find their vocations by asking: *What do I want from life?* Instead, they ask: *What is life asking of me? How can I match my intrinsic talents with the world's needs?*

As someone who was born into extreme poverty and gone on to become financially successful, I believe the formula for a good life is simple abundance without attachment. I could easily take my wealth, return to Nepal, and live like a king with my own personal doctor, cook, chauffer, body guard, and house staff. But wealth and the luxuries it provides are not what motivate me. I keep working hard because I believe I can help people and contribute to making the world a better place.

If I could leave the reader with a final offering of how the Sherpa experience might benefit Westerners, it would be this. Although I am not a practicing Buddhist like my mother and so many of her generation, I consider myself a Buddhist in thought and spirit. This includes a sense of the world as sacred. I believe a deeper spiritual engagement with the world can only help matters. This is as true on the slopes of Chomolungma as it is anywhere on earth.

In the words of a fellow Sherpa, Jamling Tenzing Norgay:

"Those who are prepared to truly see and listen will find something different, and greater, than what they were seeking. They will find that the spirit and blessings of the mountains can be found, ultimately, within us all."

ACKNOWLEDGMENTS

This book would not have been possible without the help and support of many people. I am especially indebted to the contributions of James McVey for his research and writing, Jose Yavari for the design and layout of the book, and Ann Nye West for her work in editing and permissions.

I am blessed to have known so many wonderful people in my life, beginning with my family and friends in Nepal and abroad. I especially want to recognize my brother Chhongba and my cousin Ang Temba, both of whom played an important role in my life. Thank you Nickson Mushi, Ani and Dendi, and Brot Coburn for your lasting friendship over the years.

Of course, I need to acknowledge all the people who have contributed to the success of Sherpa Ascent International, Sherpa's Adventurer Restaurant, Fuji Restaurant, and Sherpa Chai. I'd also like to thank the Colorado Mountain Club for its continuing support. I remain deeply grateful to those with whom I have worked on service projects in Nepal, most notably Ken Stober, Heather Bulk, Mike and Dhaki Salomon, and Greg Greenstreet.

Finally, I want to thank my wife Mariko and daughter Nima for their enduring love and support.

GLOSSARY

Bardo – A transitional period lasting forty-nine days in which the soul lingers close to the body before gradually moving away toward a state of reincarnation.

Beyul – Sacred, hidden valleys in the Himalayan Mountains originally set aside by Guru Rinpoche as places of peace and sanctuary for Tibetan Buddhists.

Buddha – The Indian mystic Guatama Siddartha who attained enlightenment in the sixth century B.C. The word is more commonly used to describe a being endowed with all qualities of enlightenment.

Chang – A local alcoholic drink resembling beer.

Chomolungma – The Tibetan name for Mount Everest.

Chorten – The Tibetan word for a small monument serving as a memorial for the dead. Chortens have come to symbolize the body, mind, and spiritual development of the Buddha.

Dasain – A fifteen-day ceremony celebrated by Nepalis in honor of the goddess Durga.

Duchang – A Tibetan word for "attachment," literally translated as "sticky desire."

Durga – The principal form of the Hindu goddess known as Devi or Shakti.

Dzogchen – A practice found in the Nyingma tradition that seeks to understand the nature of the mind.

Gewa – Gifts in the form of rice, butter, and money presented to well-wishers of the recently deceased. The gifts are provided by the family of the deceased to enhance the prospects of reincarnation.

Jomo Miyo Lung Sangma (goddess, mother of the earth) – Also known as Jomolungma and Chomolungma, she is the female deity who resides on Mt. Everest.

Khata – A traditional, ceremonial scarf given to greet friends, relatives, and guests to show happiness and good intentions.

Khumbila – A mountain situated in the Khumbu Valley. Khumbila is short for Khumbu-yul-lha, the protective deity of the Khumbu's land, people, and religion.

Kyetis – A large, embossed silver buckle worn by Sherpa women to hold a metil in place.

Lama – A spiritual teacher and guide.

Machikne – A Nepalese obscenity spoken to insult and show anger to another person.

Mahayana – The tradition of Buddhism practiced in the Himalayan region. The aim of Mahayana Buddhism is to attain enlightenment for all beings and promote universal compassion.

Mani Stone – Carved stones found on the landscape bearing a single chant, prayer, or Buddhist image.

Metil – A colorful, striped apron worn by Sherpa women over a togkok.

Nak – A female yak.

Nangpa La – A high mountain pass (19,050' elevation) crossing the Himalayas northwest of Khumbu along the border between Tibet and Nepal.

Nyingma – The oldest sect of Mahayana Buddhism and the source of Sherpa spirituality. The Nyingma is based on the original translations of Buddhist scriptures from Sanskrit into Old Tibetan.

Puja – A prayer ritual or act of worship practiced by Sherpas.

Rackshi – A traditional, distilled alcoholic beverage often made at home.

Rinpoche – An esteemed title reserved for high lamas and reincarnates.

Rupee – The Nepalese Rupee is the official currency of Nepal, the equivalent of just under one U.S. penny.

Sangbur – A brazier filled with burning incense used in rituals as an offering to the gods.

Sanskrit – The ancient language of India.

Sirdar – A Hindi word for a person of high rank used during the height of British rule in India when most of the siege-style Himalayan expeditions occurred.

Stupa – The Sanskrit word for chorten. Monuments that appear in a variety of forms, stupas symbolize the Buddha's enlightenment.

Terma – Hidden forms of teachings found in the Nyingma.

Togkok – A traditional long-sleeved dress worn by Sherpa women.

Yak – A large, domesticated wild ox used as a pack animal and for its meat, milk, and hide.

Yonchap – A Buddhist ritual whereby seven bowls of water are set out in the morning as an offering to the gods.

Zom – A cross between a yak and a cow.

SOURCES AND FURTHER READING

CHAPTER 1
Klatzel, Frances, *Gaiety of Spirit: The Sherpas of Everest*, Mera Publications, Kathmandu, Nepal, 2010.

CHAPTER 2
Klatzel, Frances, *Gaiety of Spirit: The Sherpas of Everest*, Mera Publications, Kathmandu, Nepal, 2010.

CHAPTER 3
Neale, Jonathan, *Tigers of the Snow: How One Fateful Climb Made the Sherpas Mountaineering Legends*, Thomas Dunne Books, St. Martin's Press, New York, 2002.

CHAPTER 5
Douglas, Ed, T*enzing, Hero of Everest*, National Geographic, Washington D.C., 2003.

Hillary, Sir Edmund, *VIEW FROM THE SUMMIT: The Remarkable Memoir by the First Person to Conquer Everest*, Copyright 1999 by Sir Edmund Hillary. Reprinted with the permission of Gallery, a division of Simon & Schuster, Inc. All rights reserved.

Kohli, M. S., *Sherpas: The Himalayan Legends*, UBS Publishers' Distributors, New Delhi, 2003.

Neale, Jonathan, *Tigers of the Snow: How One Fateful Climb Made the Sherpas Mountaineering Legends* , Thomas Dunne Books, St. Martin's Press, New York, 2002.

Peedom, Jennifer (Director), *Sherpa: Trouble on Everest*, Lion's Gate Films, 2015.

CHAPTER 7
Klatzel, Frances, *Gaiety of Spirit: The Sherpas of Everest*, Mera Publications, Kathmandu, Nepal, 2010.

Yarwood, Vaughan, *"Burra-Sahib: The Legacy of Sir Edmund Hillary,"* New Zealand Geographic Online, Issue 053, September-October 2001.

CHAPTER 8

Bhattarai, Krishna P., *Nepal*, Chelsea House Publishers, an imprint of Infobase Publishing, New York, 2008.

Whelpton, John, *A History of Nepal*, Cambridge University Press, Cambridge, United Kingdom, 2005.

CHAPTER 11

Bhattarai, Krishna P., *Nepal*, Chelsea House Publishers, an imprint of Infobase Publishing, New York, 2008.

Choegyal, Lisa and Dunham, Mikel, eds., *The Nepal Scene: Chronicles of Elizabeth Hawley 1988-2007*, Vajra Books, Kathmandu, 2015.

Sawe, Benjamin Elisha. *"What Happened During the Nepalese Civil War?"* World Atlas World Facts, www.worldatlas.com, May 16, 2018.

Whelpton, John, *A History of Nepal*, Cambridge University Press, Cambridge, United Kingdom, 2005.

CHAPTER 12

Hillary, Sir Edmund, *Schoolhouse in the Clouds*, Knopf Doubleday Penguin Random House, 1964.

Hillary, Sir Edmund, *VIEW FROM THE SUMMIT: The Remarkable Memoir by the First Person to Conquer Everest*, Copyright 1999 by Sir Edmund Hillary. Reprinted with the permission of Gallery, a division of Simon & Schuster, Inc. All rights reserved.

Yarwood, Vaughan, *"Burra-Sahib: The Legacy of Sir Edmund Hillary,"* New Zealand Geographic Online, Issue 053, September-October 2001.

CHAPTER 14

Wilkens, John, *"Building Bridges,"* San Diego Union-Tribune, July 16, 2002. E1-E3.

CHAPTER 15

Arnette, Alan, *"Everest 2014: Season Summary—A Nepal Tragedy,"* www.alanarnette.com/blog, June 9, 2014.

Peedom, Jennifer (Director), *Sherpa: Trouble on Everest*, Lion's Gate Films, 2015.

Schaffer, Grayson. *"Everest's Darkest Year,"* Outside Online. August, 2014.

Note: Russel Brice has been involved in Everest expeditions since the 1990s. In the days following the 2014 tragedy, he acted as an intermediary between government officials in Kathmandu and expedition operators and Sherpas at Base Camp. First, he sent a letter to the Nepal government requesting better working conditions for Sherpas. He then flew to Kathmandu to meet with Ministry officials, persuading a government official to fly to Base Camp to address Sherpas. Two years earlier in 2012, Brice cancelled his commercial expedition on Everest because he believed the Icefall was too dangerous.

CHAPTER 16

Adhikari, Deepak, *"Nepalese Guiding Companies Eye Everest Opportunities,"* Nikkei Asian Review, April 22, 2018.

Arnette, Alan, *"Everest 2014: Season Summary—A Nepal Tragedy,"* www.alanarnette.com/blog, June 9, 2014.

Arnette, Alan, *"Everest 2017: Adventure Consultant's Guy Cotter on 'fixing Everest','"* www.alanarnette.com/blog, March 24, 2017.

Dundruk, Master Kungga, *"Environmental Issues on Mt. Everest."* Tibet Vista, August 25, 2018.

Gunaratna, Shanika, *"The Mountain of Problems Facing Everest,"* CBSNews.com, May 26, 2016.

Gurubacharya, Binaj, *"Mount Everest Risks Contamination by a Growing Mountain of Human Waste,"* The Independent Online, March 3, 2015.

Hickock, Kimberly, *"How Much Trash Is on Everest?"* Live Science Online, July 15, 2018.

Hillary, Sir Edmund, *VIEW FROM THE SUMMIT: The Remarkable Memoir by the First Person to Conquer Everest*, Copyright 1999 by Sir Edmund Hillary. Reprinted with the permission of Gallery, a division of Simon & Schuster, Inc. All rights reserved.

Jenkins, Mark, *"Maxed out on Everest,"* NG Image Collection, National Geographic, June 2013.

Krakauer, Jon, *Into Thin Air,* Anchor Books, New York, 1997.

Peedom, Jennifer (Director), *Sherpa: Trouble on Everest*, Lion's Gate Films, 2015.

Schaffer, Grayson, *"Everest's Darkest Year,"* Outside Online. August, 2014.

CHAPTER 17

Adhikari, Narayan, *"Nepal's Earthquake Disaster: Two Years and $4.1 Bn Later,"* Al Jazeera Online, April 25, 2017.

Reid, Kathryn, *"2015 Nepal Earthquake,"* World Vision From the Field, www.worldvision.org, April 3, 2018.

Wilkinson, Freddie, *"Helicopters Rescue Climbers Trapped on Everest After Quake,"* National Geographic Online, April 27, 2015.

CHAPTER 19

Arnette, Alan, *"Everest 2014: Season Summary—A Nepal Tragedy,"* www.alanarnette.com/blog, June 9, 2014.

Douglas, Ed. *"Forget the Everest Brawl: The Real Story Is How Sherpas Are Taking Control,"* The Guardian Online, May 4, 2013.

Peedom, Jennifer (Director), *Sherpa: Trouble on Everest,* Lion's Gate Films, 2015.

Schaffer, Grayson. *"Everest's Darkest Year,"* Outside Online. August, 2014.

CHAPTER 20

Amoruso, Irene et al. *"Water-Related Environmental Public Health in Developing Countries: Installation of a Microbiology Laboratory in the Mt. Everest National Park (Nepal) and Comprehensive Training of Local Staff,"* II Congresso Nazionale CUCS sulla Cooperazione Universitaria, 2011.

Dundruk, Master Kungga, *"Environmental Issues on Mt. Everest."* Tibet Vista, August 25, 2018.

Hickock, Kimberly, *"How Much Trash Is On Mount Everest?"* Live Science Online, July 15, 2018.

Hillary, Sir Edmund, *VIEW FROM THE SUMMIT: The Remarkable Memoir by the First Person to Conquer Everest,* Copyright 1999 by Sir Edmund Hillary. Reprinted with the permission of Gallery, a division of Simon & Schuster, Inc. All rights reserved.

Massachusetts Institute of Technology, *"Clean Water for Nepal Is Focus of MIT Research,"* ScienceDaily Online, December 11, 2001.

Miller, Ryan, *"World's Highest Dump? Mount Everest Is Covered In Tons of Trash,"* USA TODAY Online, May 3, 2019.

Stern, Adam, *"More Trekkers, More Trees,"* Nepali Times, November 30, 2018.

Wootson Jr., Cleve R., Jr., *"Mount Everest is a 'fecal time bomb'. Here's one man's idea for handling 14 tons of poop,"* WashingtonPost.com, August 7, 2018.

Yarwood, Vaughan, *"Burra-Sahib: The Legacy of Sir Edmund Hillary,"* New Zealand Geographic Online, Issue 053, September-October 2001.

CHAPTER 21

Norgay, Jamling Tenzing. *"Mountains as an Existential Resource, Expression in Religion, Environment and Culture,"* Ambio, A Journal of the Human Environment, Royal Swedish Academy of Sciences, November 2004.